FIGGHIU BEDDU
Or
How I Became “Only” Alfred

Alfred M. Zappalà
Figghiu Beddu or How I Became "only" Alfred
ISBN 1881901-90-4

Cover design by Catie Rae Zappalà.

Photos: Alfred Zappalà and Vita Kazlauciunaite

For information and for orders, write to:

Legas

P.O. Box 149
Mineola, NewYork
11501, USA

3 Wood Aster Bay
Ottawa, Ontario
K2R 1D3 Canada

legaspublishing.com

Alfred M. Zappalà, esq.

FIGGHIU BEDDU

Or

How I Became "Only" Alfred

ACKNOWLEDGEMENTS

First of all, I want to thank my three children Jennifer the Wise, Matthew, and Catie Rae for allowing me to live my dream. Without their say so, I would be in Massachusetts somewhere withering away. Instead, they allowed me to move most of the year to my ancestral home of Sicily.

I also want to thank my business partner Massimo Grimaldi, my Sicilian friend and brother. The two of us have had many adventures over the years, and I am sure we will have many more. I also want to thank my friend Roberto Schiliro and his family at Café Sikelia in Naxos. A long time ago, that place entered my heart, and will always remain there.

I want to thank many of the people that I talk about in this book, one of which you will meet in many chapters, my travel colleague Vita Kazlauciunaite. Thank you is all I will say for now.

I want to thank Beth Beeman, my friend and who did all the pre-editing for me. Her comments always were insightful and spot on.

I want to thank the talented lawyer/ friend/ singer/ song writer Valerie Giglio. Her music played a huge part in my emotional re-awakening that took place somewhere in the middle of this book.

I want to thank my newsletter subscribers, all 5,000 of them and my Facebook friends, all 2,000 of them and everyone who followed my adventures in my first two books, "*The Reverse Immigrant*" and "*Gaetano's Trunk*."

I want to thank my friends in the legal education business, especially my colleagues at Northeastern University School of Law and Suffolk University School of Law which allow me the freedom to spend the rest of the year gallivanting through the Sicilian countryside.

I want to thank you too. Maybe my book will inspire you to donate to the Sicilian Project which we founded to teach English to Sicilian students and which the entire story can be found at my website. Or, maybe it will inspire you to pack your bags and come here too.

DEDICATION

To “Only” Vita….who else?
and also to
Jennifer the Wise

Two remarkable women who have taught me much.

L’AMURI D’UN FIGGHIU

I Siciliani emigrarunu cu uocchi di lacrimi chini,
Lassannu i so paisi pi destinazioni non tantu vicini,
Iddi vardavanu e fissavanu l’America luntanu assai,
e prumittevanu:”Sicilia bedda, non ti scordu mai”.
Si rignutticavanu i manichi, travagghiavanu nghiuttennu buccuni amaru,
ca parola terruni certuni li chiamaru.
Iddi si sintevanu orgogliosi di iessiri siciliani nto munnu,
Iddi avianu nu desideriu di turnari o prima o poi tantu prufunnu.
‘Ntra i Siciliani ca emigrarunu me nonna puru la so terra lassò.
Idda avissi pututu stari in america pi sempri, ma so patri in Sicilia turnò.
Uoggi n’autru figghiu di Siciliani, iu canuscii, ca rici orgogliosamenti
Ca in America nascìu, ma intra u so cori batti: “I love Sicily” sentitamenti.

Catania 7 Agosto 2012 **Rosanna De Luca**

THE LOVE OF A SON

Sicilians emigrated with eyes full of tears,
Leaving their countries for destinies not very near,
They looked and gazed far to the Americas
They promised: “Sicilia bedda non ti scordu mica.”
Rolling up the sleeves they worked,
Swallowing bitter bread, with the word “terroni.”
They were very proud to be Sicilians in the world,
They had a deep desire to come back sooner or later
Among the many Sicilians who migrated to America
my grandmother also left her country behind.
She could have stayed in America forever, but her father returned to Sicily.
Today, another Sicilian’s son I have known, says proudly
he was born in America, but inside his heart beats “I love Sicily”.

Catania August 7, 2012 **Rosanna De Luca**

Contents

In my previous two books, *The Reverse Immigrant* and *Gaetano's Trunk*, I wrote about my decision to uproot myself and move to Sicily.

A lot has happened since I made that decision. I did in fact sell my condo in Massachusetts, and I did in fact establish residency in Aci Catena, and I did in fact prove to myself that I could *reverse immigrate* back to my ancestral homeland in Sicily. And, I did this during the worse economic downturn since the Great Depression. The economic downturn now gripping Italy and Sicily, "La Crisi" as the Italians call it, surprisingly is affecting the mainland of Italy far more that Sicily.

Why is that, you ask? Well, Sicilians have been abused, vilified, oppressed, discriminated against and isolated virtually their entire history. They are survivors. That's why.

During this economic downturn, they are far better suited and better equipped to make do with less than their northern brethren. The spirit of "never say die" lives on.

Plus, the mafia has been eviscerated in Sicily.

Yes, the mafia still exists, but most of the big shots are dead or in jail for life. The Calabrian mafia, the Neapolitan mafia, and other mafias have filled the void, but legitimate businesses are now growing without the mafia breathing down their necks. Only residual pockets remain, and the spirit of Falcone and Borsellino burn bright with the young working professionals. As the population gets more conversant in English and better educated, the lingering stench of the mafia will lessen even more.

And for me?

I have found emotional tranquility. And I finally have started a new meme in life. As my health permits, and so far it has been so good, I will continue on as *"only Alfred"* for a while. If the right person comes along, I will create a new meme. However, being surrounded with so many people who love me both here and in America, emotionally I am on bonus time now.

I wrote this book from the heart. I hope you enjoy it.

Alfred M. Zappalà

www.alfredzappala.com
Aci Catena, Sicily
October, 2012

Note: I have posted hundreds of photos of the people and places mentioned in this book on my blog *www.alfredmzappala.blog.com* for you to enjoy as well.

Chapter One

Prologue

1. A Prolonged Out of Mind Experience

Three years ago, I got this hair-brained idea that I should sell all my possessions, alter my life completely and forever, and move to Sicily. At the time, it was simply an idea, something to aspire to after I hit the lottery. After all, I had just turned sixty years old and geezers my age are supposed to play golf with their friends and go to Florida for the winter.

Not me.

I decided that Sicily was where I wanted to be. I had experienced a metamorphosis the first time I had visited Sicily and the call to return was overwhelming and unyielding. I was going to move to Sicily no matter what. Not only was I going to move to Sicily, I would record my thoughts, write of my adventures, and generally have a paradigm change in my life.

Most of my friends thought I was out of my mind. While most of them thought the idea a neat one, not too many took me seriously. Except of course, my children, who encouraged me to chase my dream. With their support and backing and knowing that the airplane flew both ways across the Atlantic if I ever had a change of heart, I stepped-up my plans to make the leap.

Except for the outbreak of World War I, the Great Depression of the 1930s, and World War II, I do not think I could have picked a worse time to make this decision.

The world economy had fallen apart, the euro was very strong against the dollar, and worse, the US economy had pretty much wiped me out financially. Not only that, I found out during this time frame that I had a heart problem and had to have stents placed into my heart.

Let's see, bad economic times, wiped out financially by the economy, and a health problem rearing its head at exactly the wrong moment. Hmm. Maybe the more prudent decision would have been to keep these plans in the recesses of my brain and fly off to Florida and grab the nightly special at Food Court.

Nope. That wasn't going to happen to me. "Carpe Diem" as they say. "Better to live one day as a lion than the rest of your life as a lamb" as Machiavelli said. Or as my son Matthew used to say, "What is the worst case, dad? If you bust out in Sicily and return penniless, all we will do is put you in a nursing home." Ha-ha, very funny.

While my son was simply busting my chops a bit with his off-kilter humor, he was really saying to me "Go ahead, dad, do it. Nothing ventured, nothing gained. You are a survivor, you are smart as hell, and you will figure it out. If anyone can pull this off, you can."

Actually, he was 100% correct. My grandfathers Gaetano Torrisi and Alfio Zappala had come to America with no money, no English skills, no place to live, no education, little support system, and a myriad other insurmountable obstacles and had made it very nicely. If they could do it against all odds, so could I.

Actually, the one thing I do have, (and still do), is my unflappable faith in my Lord, Jesus Christ. We became re-acquainted as I lay in the hospital recovering from the two stents installed by the doctors from Saint Elizabeth's in Boston. My Augustinian, Jesuit and Franciscan theology education that I had received had come and lifted my soul.

While I did not know what the future held for me, I now knew who held it.

Not only that, but people were hearing about what I was going to do, and they contacted me every day with words of encouragement. Strangers who knew me only through my newsletter, my blog or my books contacted me. Yup, I was going to do this.

Thus, with lint in my pocket, a bottle of heart pills in my satchel, and armed only with 100% Sicilian guile and the ability that has been genetically implanted in me by a millennia of my forefathers, I made the decision that not only was this a good idea, but one that I was 10000% sure was the correct one.

Maybe.

Thus, getting up off the ground, dusting myself off, I re-entered the fray. This time, I would do it.

How, I do not know, but I intended to give it my best shot.

2. Organizational Considerations

One thing that I learned the last few years is that you cannot just hop on a plane and say you are going to move to a foreign country. Well, you can say that, but in practical reality you will be heading home in short order for some reason or another. A move to another country requires planning, preparation, and gumption no matter how well intentioned the thoughts are to become one with your culture.

I found out the hard way that many steps are required in the process.

Fortunately, before I made the decision to stop my life in America and U-turn it to Sicily, some of the major big stuff inadvertently had been accomplished. The most important being, of course, was me obtaining Italian citizenship "*de jure sangis*."

What this means is that I became an Italian citizen through blood. When both my grandfathers came to America long ago, they had children in America BEFORE they themselves had become American citizens and they did not renounce their Italian citizenship. Thus, in my father's case, under Italian law, he was the son of an Italian citizen, and since my dad was an Italian citizen, I was too as the son of an Italian citizen.

I recall having a lot of fun, as well as intrigue many years ago as I located documents in Sicily and wound through the process of Italian citizenship.

I located all sorts of interesting documents along the way as I recall, and I was indeed pleased the day that I was contacted by the Italian authorities and told that I can make an appointment for getting my Italian passport. Of course, an added benefit of Italian citizenship is European citizenship, although in light of the current economy in Europe that may or may not be a good idea. Nonetheless, with the red-covered European passport in my possession I was assured that if in fact I chose to ever live in Italy, I would have none of the visa issues, immigration issues, or red-tape issues that foreigners have. Nope, I was an Italian citizen and could live anyplace in Italy that I wished.

With the citizenship issue solved, the next questions were, of course (a) where will you live, (b) how will you live and (c) can you sustain yourself living there?

In my previous two books about my adventures in Sicily, *The Reverse Immigrant* and *Gaetano's Trunk*, I had decided to live on the east coast of Sicily, close to my ancestral village of Trecastagni. Trecastagni is a beautiful little mountain town located on the slope of Mt. Etna, and I chose the beautiful village of Aci Catena to set up my permanent residence.

I had several other locations that I first experimented with, but Aci Catena was close the Ionian Sea which I need to replenish my spirit on a daily basis, yet close to the autostrada so I can zip here and there. Having a decent place to live is the second requirement, along with many of the amenities that I was used to in America.

I was going native but I was going American-Sicilian native. I am very proud of my America citizenship and background, so I am a hybrid in a special sort of way. Thus, over time, I furnished my place with things like computers, office work space, American kitchen gadgets that I love, an iPod, CD players and things that my grandfathers would only scratch their heads about.

In short, I was a twenty-first century immigrant, with a twentieth century body that blended the best of two cultures into a special type of Italian. I was very happy about that!

Having a place to live along with my passport was crucial. The only remaining major item that I had to solve was the "how," as in how was I expected to support myself? That was the $65,000 question that needed to be answered as my dad used to say, and I had been mulling this issue long before I had made the initial decision to uproot myself and move to Sicily.

3. The "How"

A wise man once told me: "Kid, you want to make money? That's easy. Do what you do best and keep doing it."

One thing I wasn't going to do in Sicily, especially at my age, was to open a pizzeria or a bed and breakfast. My strength was that of a negotiator, an attorney, a teacher and a writer. Thus, I decided to focus on my skills and simply re-direct them to Sicily. I would practice law in Sicily with my Sicilian law partner Massimo, negotiate important deals on behalf of my clients, teach people about Sicily through my

Sicilian newsletter, and write about Sicily. I would take that old man's advice; I would do what I do best and keep on doing it.

The most important decision that I made, however, was to decide to return to America for several months at a time to teach law and re-fill my meager bank account…just in case.

Thus, I did have a plan after all. I just had to see it.

A new piece was added, however. In Sicily I very much enjoyed spending time in Naxos at the Café Sikelia with my friend Roberto and his sisters Sonya, Maria Grazia, and Nancy. (Of course, any red-blooded man of any sensibility would enjoy spending time with this family. The sisters are the epitome of Sicilian beauty and charm). However, I found out that I enjoyed helping the family when the Americans were on holiday and stopped at their Café, which is really a terrific outdoor restaurant.

Thus, I inadvertently fell into the tourist business as well and actually coordinated several trips to Sicily. However, if you take a step back and examine all the trees in the forest that I had assembled in order to answer the "how" of how was I going to support myself, everything was generally related to one thing: my love of Sicily. I concluded, therefore, that I would and could pull it off.

4. Shedding Personal History

Carlos Castellaneda, who wrote some very interesting books back in my hippie-college days in Boston and Maine in the early 1970s, especially in his book *The Teachings of Don Juan*, often said that the first step is to shed personal history.

Don't look over your shoulder, he counseled.

After I had my kids and grandkids I realized that he was full of baloney. There was no way in hell that I would ever forget my family. He was, I concluded, a nut case. My family was my life and my reason for getting up in the morning. However, he did have something there if you factored out the family. If he meant get rid of everything else except the family, I agree.

Which is exactly what I did.

Over a six-month period, I literally gave away, sold, or disposed of a life time of personal history in America.

My kids had first dibs on everything. They chose what they wanted and they hauled it away. Craig's List had second dibs. I sold what I could. The charities had third dibs, and I also donated a lot of things. Finally, the garbage man had his chance too. And, what about me? Whatever I really wanted to use on a daily basis, I threw into my suitcase. The balance of what I wanted, after sorting, culling, eliminating, and streamlining, went into exactly twenty plastic storage tubs stored now at my daughter Jen's house.

As I stepped on the plane to Sicily a scant one week ago, I clearly remembered that when I returned in the fall to teach law at my beloved law schools that I would be essentially a homeless person in America.

But you know what? Just like James Earl Jones did in my favorite film with Kevin Costner called *Field of Dreams,* giggling all the while as he stuck his hand in and out of the stalks of corn before entering paradise, I was doing the same thing. Nothing could keep me from smiling as I prepared to enter my paradise.

My "*Field of Dreams*" was Sicily and not a ball field. My paradise has and always will be La Sicilia. Thus, with personal history eliminated, stored and deleted, I stepped on the Alitalia jet to Sicily as I had so many times. Except this time it was different. It was with a sense of adventure. That's the fun part of life, isn't it? *Carpe Diem*, right? The grand adventure had begun.

Chapter Two

Arrival

1. The Landing Zone

I was really looking forward to getting to Sicily this time.

This trip would be the litmus test, the ultimate survival test. I had scrimped and saved all winter long and had gathered enough cash to live in Sicily for six months if I didn't earn a dime. That wasn't the plan though. The plan was to earn dimes and to earn enough of them so that I wouldn't have to touch my little nest egg.

One thing that studying two thousand years of Sicilian history has taught me is that Sicilians are survivors, overcoming obstacles throughout history that would have pushed a lesser gene pool into oblivion.

Fortunately, I was blessed with a healthy dose of those survivor genes. My only limitation was what I could not put on myself. One year ago I had discovered that I was not Hercules and that a high-stress, high-energy life has, over time, severe consequences. In my case it was two stainless steel micro stents that were placed in my heart by the good doctors at Saint Elizabeth's hospital in Boston in order to re-open two heart arteries that had shut down.

A winter spent in cardiac rehabilitation, nutritional discovery and shedding of bad habits that slowly led up to this near catastrophic experience was still rattling in the back of my head. If I was to pull this off and re-locate to a completely different environment, I had to be healthy…or at least functional.

A check with my cardiologist and a series of blood work confirmed to me that my health would not be a problem as long as I paced myself and didn't over-do it. My grandfather Gaetano's words of "everything in moderation" would be my mantra.

I had eliminated almost all (note I said almost all) red meat from my diet. Every once in awhile I treated myself to a morsel of meat just to remember how carnivores once lived. But, for the most part, red meat was no longer in my diet.

Almost all fried foods were gone too. Salt was dispatched from my life, as were a nasty cigarette habit, processed foods, fast foods and heavy deserts. Almost overnight, at my late age, I was getting healthier. To be honest, since the cardiac event over one year ago, I looked and felt light years better. My body and my mind, I decided, would be able to function properly in Sicily.

As would my car.

My little pride and joy, a (greatly) used 2000 Fiat Punto five speed with probably 150,000 miles on it, was all bought and paid for. It wasn't much to look at, but it got me from point A to point B in an efficient and economical manner. It would later be dubbed "The Magic Carpet" by me.

With gasoline prices hitting nearly nine dollars a gallon in Sicily this year, a gas-sipping automobile is a valuable friend. The Magic Carpet and I were now fast friends.

And it was the same with the young couple that had rented the spare bedroom upstairs in my house in Aci Catena. Their 400-euro a month rent that they chipped in helped pay for the natural gas used to heat the house, the skyrocketing electricity bill, and the cable bill.

Finally, after a two-year wait, ASDL internet cable was available in our area. It wasn't the fast broadband that I had in the states, but a quantum improvement over past years.

Necessities such as a washing machine, dining room set, kitchen set, pots and pans, flatware, and all the other things I needed to live modestly had been slowly purchased over the years. My place in Aci Catena was now fully equipped to satisfy my American-instilled sense of what was necessary to survive.

As for the young couple who shared some of the expenses, they were happy that they had found me. Rest assured that the existence that I had gathered for myself in Sicily, far less than what I had in America by a factor of twenty, was a cause of joy for them. Simply put, they could never afford the living environment that I had created. However, it was time for them to spread their wings and shortly after I would arrive, they would move into their own place.

While modest by any American standard, it became apparent to me now that while things were tough …it would be manageable.

2. The Reality of the Situation.

For the last five years, virtually every time I have returned to Sicily, things had gotten worse.

The economic disaster that gripped the world has hit Italy hard, and Sicily even harder. As the poor step-child of Italy, the Sicilians have long learned that the money earmarked for them in Rome somehow never hit the intended destination. By the time those financial earmarks do hit Sicily, once the monies have been picked over by everyone and their brother, almost nothing is left for those who need it.

Thus, a flight of sorts is once again taking place.

This time, however, it is not the un-educated who fled Sicily by the hundreds of thousands in they did in the early 20th century. This time it is the *critical intellectual mass* of young college grads. It is they who cannot find a job, cannot afford a place to rent (home ownership is seemingly a dream now except for the wealthy), cannot afford anything except a non-guaranteed job without the almighty contract that would guarantee a worker basic employment rights.

An economy that cannot compete within the European Union because of terrible language skills assures Sicily its place, along with Greece, Spain and Portugal as Europe's economic laggards.

The two millennia beat down of the downtrodden Sicily continues except that the educated are now fleeing. How about the uneducated? Sadly, they are left to fend on their own.

With this in mind, I adopt the mindset of a first responder. As others flee the fire, still others run toward it in the hopes of rescue. One man can do nothing. But one man who can trumpet the warning, who can talk and who can see, and most importantly who can herald what is happening, could possibly be a valuable asset indeed.

But, to whom?

That is the easiest answer of all - to the twelve million Sicilian-Americans who claim their blood from Sicily. For today, you see, there are twice as many Sicilian-Americans as there are Sicilians themselves, twelve million in America compared to five and a half million who live today in Sicily.

The answer therefore becomes obvious. The solution lies across the sea in the United States. Thus my adventure that begins again today is one of enlightenment aided by my ability to write, to social network, and to yell from the mountaintops: "Sicily needs us!"

So I shall start to enlighten, to teach, to entertain, to plead, and to inform all of you about my Sicily, our Sicily. It will be truly an excellent ride!

Chapter Three

Behold the Noble Fava

Since ancient Greek and Roman times, Sicilians have been connected to the fava bean. It is a staple of Sicilian cuisine and perhaps was done an injustice by Hannibal Lecter in the film *Silence of the Lambs* when he suggested a nice glass of Chianti as an unlikely pairing.

I prefer the *vino rosso locale*, especially at the current price of about 1.85 euro (roughly $2.50 USD) per liter. Fava and vino, the nectar of the Gods!

In reality, the noble fava has done quite a bit to assure the survival of the Sicilian species over the millennia. A family of five in Sicily can be fed a delicious, nutritious and healthy meal of fava for under five dollars!

Think about that. If you throw in a loaf of bread and a glass of wine, what else is there to life?

Fava beans, I am told by those in the know are really members of the pea family, and not members of the bean family. In a hot climate such as Sicily they grow throughout the spring and summer and their ground spread offers vital protection for the Sicilian soil.

Fava plants spread out, not up, preserving the topsoil. Thus, this environmentally friendly bean provides tremendous value to the Sicilian people.

The health benefits of the fava are well known too. They are low in total fat, low in saturated fat, high in protein and high in fiber. The noble fava bean packs quite a health punch indeed.

It is with this in mind that yesterday I visited my friend Agatha, the owner of a local green grocer. The spring's first crop was now available and I intended to buy a kilo of fava in order to make my favorite health dish of all, Alfred's Fava Bean Delight.

Agatha's place is not a big place. It doesn't have to be. Fruits and vegetables are meticulously displayed in wooden crates slightly tilted toward the consumer and protected under a wonderful awning. She has three displays of products, leafy vegetables on one side, fruits in the middle and beans, tomatoes, potatoes, broccoli, and cauliflower on the other.

Looking at the fruits my mouth watered. The peaches, plums, cherries, gelsi (mulberries), and fragole (strawberries) from Etna were just picked and the fragrances drove me wild. The color of each fruit was intense. I really could not take my eyes off of them.

Since I buy my fruit daily, I selected two peaches, a small box of the fantastic tiny strawberries from Etna, and a double handful of ruby-red cherries. Fresh fruit is a great substitute for me whenever I get the craving for something sweet, and I eat fruit throughout the day.

Today though, I was on the hunt for fava, and I found them. Agatha had just received a supply from the local grower and these babies were nothing to sneeze at. Each stalk was roughly eight inches long and nearly one and a half inches wide. They were spectacular to behold.

Their slightly curved shape and rich green color made me believe that these would be the finest fava meal ever. The only drawback that I could see was the fact that I had to shell them, which for me was a giant pain. Not that shelling is hard work, quite the opposite. However, it was time consuming and in my eagerness to devour these babies, I would have to shell them first.

Or so I thought.

"Alfredo" said Agatha. "I have a kilo all cleaned. Would you prefer these?" she asked.

"Grazie, Agatha." I said. "Yes, I would…you knew I was coming, didn't you?" I said.

"Well, this is how you always buy them so I now have a few kilos put aside for others too!" she said as she handed me a bag "Would you like the peas and onion too?"

No Sicilian in his right mind would make fava without the companions of fresh peas and sweet onion, and sure enough, a nice bag of freshly shelled peas was ready and waiting for me too!

Thus I now had in my possession the three prime ingredients for a delectable meal. A quick stop at the panificio (bread maker) for a small loaf of freshly made crusty bread and I was well on the way to culinary heaven.

This meal was shaping up to be legendary especially since the vino that Agatha had sold me was as "stupendo" as she said.

Bread, wine, fresh fruits and fava…I do not think I could be happier.

When I got home, I set the mood. Today was an Adriano Celentano day. Celentano was the Italian equivalent to Frank Sinatra, and somehow in my mind he is associated with cooking. I always play Celentano when I prepare food.

The first thing I did was to pour myself a glass of the vino locale, just to make sure it was good. Of course it was good! That was just a flimsy excuse that I love to make. It seems to work every time I use it!

I pulled out my sauce pan and put it on the stove. The first thing I did was peel the onion and dice it up. I lit the fire under the burner and let them sweat a little. I added in olive oil, not too much, maybe 3 tablespoons, and a little salt and pepper, and then added the fava and the peas.

I usually do a 2-1 ratio (twice the amount of fava to peas). I added in a half glass of water and let those babies cook over a medium heat. As the water dissipated, I added in another half glass of water and cooked them until almost all the water was gone. I stirred constantly with a wooden spoon.

Keeping an eyeball on this treasure as I stirred, after about 10 to twelve minutes, the fava were done. They had absorbed the water and were almost as big as a quarter. I shut the fire off and let them sit.

The secret to enjoying fava is eating them tepid, at room temperature. I let 10 minutes pass.

Scooping out a healthy portion of the fava and peas, I sprinkled a little freshly grated cheese on top, and a little more black pepper. Refilling my glass with the required second glass of vino rosso and ripping off a good chuck of bread, I sat down to enjoy my feast.

While I know that fava is served in many countries including the United States, I can say that a bowl of fava is meant to be eaten in this manner and only in one place…at my table…in my house… and in Sicily!

Chapter Four

Sicilian Cinderella

Last night I witnessed a transformation of a woman before my eyes that still has me talking to myself.

I know what I saw, but I do not believe it. I experienced a magical moment in an ancient city watching something that I never imagined I would be watching. And it really floored me.

Here is the story:

My friend Antonia invited me to attend a tango lesson with her and her boyfriend Alessandro at their tango school, Scuola di Danza di Maria Patti, in Catania.

Me? A tango lesson? Mr. Twinkle-Toes? Sure, why not I said.

Besides inviting me, she had also invited our other friends Maria and Alessio. Antonia and Alessandro had been taking lessons for about a year every Sunday night at the studio. Although I sensed that Alessandro wasn't particularly enthused about the weekly trip around the dance floor, he dutifully fulfilled his obligation as a boyfriend every Sunday night just to keep the peace.

This particular evening was an open house at the school for all who were thinking of taking tango lessons. Antonia had invited Maria and Alessio in the hope that they would be enamored with the night and take lessons themselves. Judging from Alessio's grumbling I thought the chances were slim of that happening right off the bat.

Nonetheless, about fifty curious couple of all ages, shapes and sizes had shown up in order to learn a few basic moves.

Antonia and Alessandro had been taking tango lessons for about one year and I could tell she really liked the night out. She talked about her teachers Antonella and Massimiliano and how they had studied "Tango di Argentina" in Argentina and that were two of Sicily's best dancers.

Two of the best Sicilian Argentinean tango dancers who studied in Argentina? How many of them could there possibly be in Sicily I kept asking myself. Didn't these two win by default? Not wanting to be a complete killjoy, I pretended to be interested the entire ride into Catania that evening and was prepared to be bored out of my mind.

For Catania, the school was in surprisingly great shape.

It was large, airy and new. The space was arranged nicely with several large rooms with different types of dance floors depending on what group was taking lessons that day. There was a practice area for ballerinas, another for ball-room-dancers and still a larger one for tango dancers.

Because the event had been advertised in *La Sicilia*, the regional newspaper, and since free refreshments were being offered (which was also advertised), a fair number of people had shown up simply to munch on the chips, drink Coke, and watch the activities.

A very popular television show (that actually started in Italy first and was later picked up by American television) named *Ballando con le Stelle* (Dancing with the Stars) had made dancing popular again in Sicily.

While dancing has always been popular in Sicily, especially salsa dancing, the television program had ignited a national craze and dance studios were popping up everywhere. Antonia's was the biggest and the best as she told me several hundred times.

Upon arrival, Antonella and Massimiliano greeted people and had everybody sign a sign-in sheet so they could be later contacted and talked into taking tango lessons. They were both elegant, although Massimiliano looked a little silly in a John Travolta type of silk shirt that was unbuttoned almost half way down his chest.

Nonetheless, thinking that was the way it was with Sicilian tango dancers who studied tango in Argentina, I smiled and filled out the form and moved down the greeting line and handed it to a rather frumpy looking woman with closely cropped hair and a boxy body type.

Strange, I thought to myself. No way is this woman a dance teacher. She must be the secretary of something, I thought to myself.

"Buona sera" she said. "Mi chiamo Paola". Ok, I said to myself, the secretary's name is Paula.

Moving into the large dance area where the lesson was to take place, we milled around exchanging small talk, and this gave me an opportunity to see who was in the crowd.

The first thing I noticed was that everyone was nicely dressed. There were no jeans, no sneakers, and no shorts. Women were nicely dressed and the men had on slacks and a nice shirt, and everyone had on decent shoes. This is the way of Sicily. *Bella figura*. Only tourists wear shorts and sneakers around town. The only acceptable place for such clothing is the beach, that's it. Tonight was no exception.

The dance teachers turned the dance lights on and walked to the center of the dance floor. With a microphone in hand, Antonella and Massimiliano thanked everyone for coming and proceeded to show a few basic moves.

In no time at all, the entire crowd was moving around the dance floor doing the two basic steps that they had been taught.

For about one hour the lesson continued. First they would show a dance step or two, and then the whole crowd would try the step. The instructors went around and corrected people.

I quickly decided that the tango was not for me and I became an observer. I was enjoying the look of pleasure on just about every woman's face as they twirled around the dance floor and the look of almost complete resignation with their accompanying dance partners.

Actually it was a comical juxtaposition. The things men do, I thought to myself, in order to keep the peace!

For the last segment, the instructors then told the crowd that two students would demonstrate a complete tango dance. With this announcement, the crowd hushed in anticipation. All the basic moves that they had gone over for the last hour were now were going to be tied together in a complete dance by two students. I was curious to see this and leaned forward to watch the activity.

To my complete and utter shock, the boxy and frumpy "assistant" Paola stepped forth with this incredibly handsome guy.

With the playing of the first note of a very sexy tango dance tune that played over the speaker system, Paola instantly became transformed from this frumpy-boxy secretary type woman into a sensual, attractive and elegant creature.

The music and she became one.

She, not her dance partner became the center of attraction. As she kicked her legs back and forth, as she effortlessly glided around the floor twirling here, twirling there, in perfect harmony with the incredibly sexy music, everyone in the room became transfixed on what they were seeing.

I could not take my eyes off this woman for what seemed like an hour. In reality, the dance lasted only several minutes and that was it. But believe me when I tell you it lasted an hour.

She was elegant, alive, glowing, beautiful, sexy, enchanted.... until the music stopped.

Then, she transformed back to her previous self.

Tango, I later found out, was Paola's life. She was indeed a secretary. She was forty years old, single and lived in an apartment with her mother.

Antonia told me that a man had broken her heart and left her at the altar, and that she had married dance and that was her love in life. Sunday nights were the most important night of the week for her. She lived for that transformation, however brief, that took place as she danced the Argentinian tango in that dance studio in Catania.

That dance floor was Paola's world. I will never forget what I saw that night.

I was told that forty new students signed up for lessons that night. I know why too. It had nothing to do with the instructors.

Rather it had everything to do with and ordinary and plain women who became the Sicilian Cinderella very briefly that evening and had captivated the soul and imagination of everyone who had watched her and shared her shared that brief experience. It was now seared into our collective minds forever.

It was a truly remarkable evening with a Sicilian Cinderella and a night I will never forget.

Chapter Five

La Festa Della Mamma

Sicilian moms are a special breed. Their life paradigm changes the day their first child is born as they re-focus their existence on their bambino.

As more children arrive, the plural "bambini" kick in.

While some women in Sicily have traditional large families of three, four, five children or more, the current economic condition in Europe the past decade has gradually reduced that number. Today, a one or two child family is the norm. The biggest difference the last decade, however, is the amount of women that are forced to enter the workplace, as a single-earner family just can't seem to make it.

Sicilian moms are now very much like American working moms, juggling a million things every day and silently sacrificing themselves for their family. I learned long ago that the female gender is truly the stronger gender and tip my cap at the dedication that Sicilian women (and women everywhere, really) show to their children.

Yesterday was La Festa Della Mamma, Mother's Day in Sicily.

The day was a gorgeous sun -filled day, and as the mid-May Sicilian sunshine kissed the entire Island, I decided to take my morning walk in Acicastello by the Norman Castle. Sundays in Acicastello usually meant that special activities would be planned. I was curious as to see if any special Mother's Day activities were going on.

Driving The Magic Carpet into town I found my usual parking space that is one of the few free parking spaces in town. The Sicilian authorities have discovered an excellent way to raise revenue. Not only do they charge for parking (typically 2 euro for four hours), but they zealously ticket every car that does not have that little scratch-ticket on the inside by the steering wheel that signifies that a parking ticket was, in fact, purchased.

In Sicily, there are no parking meters per se (they would disappear very quickly, I think!). Rather, you must purchase a parking scratch ticket at the bar or tobacco shop and place it inside your car by the steering wheel. Meter maids then go around and write tickets for scofflaws. On Sundays, meter maids are everywhere, so to know where to park for free is a profound accomplishment

After I parked my car I noticed a long line of children dressed in Cub Scout, Brownie, Boy Scout, Girl Scout, and Explorer uniforms marching double file down the street.

They were arranged by age, with the little one (six, seven, and eight year olds) marching in the front and the progressively older ones marching further behind. It was truly a splendid sight and I could not recall seeing such a thing in the recent past in America. The faces were freshly scrubbed, the uniforms pressed and clean, and everyone was singing a marching song. I stood to the side as they passed by and was reminded of a by-gone era in America. I fell in behind the group as they headed to the Norman Castle. I wanted to see what they were going to do.

As we got closer to the Castle, I heard music and saw a group of women dancing in the shadows of the Castle. The Commune had constructed tents and a fitness instructor was conducting a free workout for any who wished to join. About fifty children, teens, and adults…all female…were enjoying themselves as they worked out to pulsating salsa music lead by the enthusiastic instructor.

Off to the side, balloon vendors were selling balloons and other children's inflatable toys. Another group of vendors was selling hand-made jewelry and the like, and the piazza was lined with many locals selling things…all for mom.

The Boy Scouts and Girl Scouts were set up too in a giant tent selling flowers and plants for mom. I found out that this was part of a yearlong- planned fund raising activity for the various troops. All year they learned about plants and flowers and had actually potted and grew them to be sold on this day.

Not far away, families were sitting at one of the many outside *gelaterie*, eating that wonderful frozen concoction brought to Sicily by the Saracens a millennia ago called granita (pronounced

gra-nee-ta) or licking a wonderful gelato. Granita is a distant relative to American slush or Italian ices except five thousand times better…truly a delicious treat on such a wonderful day.

As I walked around the piazza, the one central theme that struck me this day was the strong sense of family that I was seeing. The thought brought me back to a simpler time long ago in America on a warm spring day when my mom and dad would also do such things with me and my brother and sister on Mother's Day.

I am happy that I was able to experience La Festa Della Mamma in Sicily this year.

I think it was a wonderful glimpse into the average Sicilian family and taught me yet again the important role that mother's truly have in maintaining the family unit and how their families really appreciate their work.

Men sometime do not show the true depth of their feelings to women. They lack emotional intelligence as a gender to do so. But on a day like today, even men realize that women are the central component of the family.

I hope they do, anyway!

Chapter Six

Stranger in a Strange Land

Yesterday was one of those days that I wanted to be alone and slip on my persona of a "Stranger in a Strange Land". Every once in a while I do this, just take off for the day and observe people. I learn the most about life this way.

I had promised friends that I would go to Taormina in order to take some photos for them. One of my friends wanted a photo of an Irish couple that was getting married at the Chiesa di San Giuseppe. They had flown here from Dublin along with their wedding party.

Another asked that I take a picture of her favorite bar in Taormina, a pretty famous watering hole named Billy&Billy and its famous owner, the elegant and beautiful Giusy. Slipping on my man-bag (these things are so handy…they can carry a lot of stuff, plus I get to feel like Brad Pitt who also has one), and throwing my camera and back-up batteries in the bag, along with my cell phone and iPod, I jumped into my car and headed into Taormina.

The day was clear and bright but a little windy. I decided to take the shore road from Acitrezza to Taormina as I loved winding my way through the little villages like Mascali, Giarre, and Fiumefreddo and into Naxos before heading into Taormina. Plus, using this route I save 1.30 euro in tolls! The plan was to take a leisurely ride and stop here and there in order to take photos of my favorite places so I could post them on Facebook as many of my friends were now following my daily activities and enjoyed my posts about living in Sicily.

I took some great shots of the port of Naxos from the top of the hill heading up to Taormina and also of Isola Bella, perhaps the most picturesque beach in all of Sicily.

I decided to park my car at the public lot and take the Funivia (tram) up the hill to Taormina and enjoy the sights. There were Germans, Austrians, Russians and Swiss waiting for the tram. I was the only English-speaker and I enjoyed the giggles of excitement as they piled into the tramcar and headed up the mountain for the short two-minute ride up the mountain.

Tourists were everywhere when we disembarked and I melted into the crowd.

I loved watching people and in fact saw people from all walks of life. I saw Sicilian school children on a field trip with their teachers and the chaperones that had them holding hands as they walked up the Corso Umberto. I saw old men and women from the from town sitting on the benches catching up on the news of the day, foreigners from Europe and Asia and tour guides leading packs of tourists focused more on licking their gelatos than taking in the beauty of this ancient and historic setting. I also saw a thousand other sights, sounds and textures that make Taormina so very special to me.

I just love this place.

I took my time walking up the Corso Umberto as I window shopped to see the latest styles in men's and women's fashions. All the famous brands have shops here. I peered into the jewelry shops, souvenir shops, gift shops, art galleries and before I knew it, an hour and a half had past.

I had been lost in paradise so I hurried to the Piazza Nove Aprile to have an espresso at the Wunderbar and wait for the wedding party that I had come to photograph.

Then something strange occurred.

While waiting for the wedding party to emerge from the church, a funeral procession slowly walked down the Corso.

First the hearse, followed on foot by the grieving family, and followed by the grieving friends. Just like the old films I had seen.

Here, in Taormina on this glorious day, a funeral procession marched by me as I sipped an espresso at the Wunderbar. Strangely, I felt out of sorts and a tad uncomfortable.

It seemed that an old timer had died. The grieving wife walked alone, assisted only by her adult children. A serious end of life scene was being played out before my eyes in the playground of Europe.

After the procession had passed, I tried to process what I had just witnessed. As I was re-playing the scene in my mind, I looked up to the church and saw its doors opening and the wedding party emerge. One hundred meters down the Corso Umberto were the remnants of the funeral procession, and now a wedding party was about to follow its path.

As I saw this unfolding, my mind wondered how often this occurred over time. Funeral processions, wedding parties, and perhaps other types of processions, time and time again over these ancient streets probably happened every day. From Greek to Roman to Saracen to Norman to Spanish to modern day Sicilian, all grieving and or celebrating something or other.

The wedding party proceeded down the Corso only fifty meters and entered a nearby restaurant, oblivious to everything except their celebration. The bride was young and beautiful and the husband handsome. Their life had barely begun and the best years still lay in front of them.

They had a family to bring up and the joys and sadness and successes and failures of life still had to unfold for them, but for this day nothing else mattered but their wedding celebration.

I took some photos and later posted them on Facebook for my friends. I wished, though, that I had taken some photos of that funeral procession. Those images, I decided, were far more profound to me on this day.

The juxtaposition of end of life and then a new life just beginning on the Corso Umberto just as it had for two millennia in Taormina. It was truly a lesson in life for me on this glorious and warm day.

Taormina…truly the Pearl of Europe…always.

Chapter Seven

The Dream of Dual Citizenship

About fifteen years ago, I became an Italian citizen. I have to tell you that I am really happy that I did. It has helped me tremendously re-discover my cultural identity and made my decision far easier to re-locate to Sicily.

I had no visa issues am proud of my Italian citizenship.

When I decided to formally declare residency in Sicily last year, the process was seamless and without pain or frustration, which was a huge surprise to me given how there always seems to be a problem with everything here.

Of course, I remain a proud American citizen too, and will never give up "Big Blue", my American passport.

America to me is my safe haven and my birth land, the land where my family resides and I will be forever grateful to her. In Sicily, I pretty much wear my Americanism on my sleeve, and people seem to respect me for it, truth be told. Sicilians love Americans.

Since I am a hybrid of sorts, I have the best of both worlds.

So can you.

If you are contemplating Italian citizenship, first you must see if you qualify for citizenship, and if you do, the process can be fun and fulfilling.

To be considered a dual citizen *jure sanguinis*, you must quality for citizenship by continuity of blood.

For example, if your father was an Italian citizen when you were born and if you never renounced your right to Italian citizenship, then you are an Italian citizen! In the same vein, if your mother was an Italian citizen at the time of your birth and you were born after January 1, 1948, and you never renounced the right to Italian citizenship, then you are also an Italian citizen and are considered a dual citizen!

To formalize the process, you must gather up various documents such as birth, death and naturalization certificates, marriage licenses, along with an apostille and original documents such as birth, marriage, death documents from the town that you are claiming lineage, and they must be presented to the Italian Consulate in the jurisdiction in which you live.

This hasn't always been the case.

Jure sanguinis has been around only since 1992, when the Italian government passed a law (no. 91, art. 11) stating that any Italian citizen who acquired or reacquired a foreign citizenship after August 15, 1992 would not lose his or her Italian citizenship.

About 5000 Americans annully apply for dual citizenship. It is a drop in the bucket from the thirty million Americans who can claim Italian ancestry of some sort.

There are many benefits of Italian citizenship. First, as an Italian citizen, you can vote in local and national elections (yes, if you are a US citizen, you can vote in the US as well!).

And, you can also pass on your citizenship to your children.

A big difference is that as opposed to all the vitriol in America regarding universal health coverage for its citizens, in Italy, there is free access to public health care. As for a college education, that is free as well, although there is an additional tax (which is very modest) for those enrolled at public universities.

Since Italy is a member of the European Union, as an Italian citizen you can work or live in any EU country without having to worry about being an illegal alien or undocumented worker. Article 17 (ex Article 8) of the Treaty on the European Union tells us that any person holding the nationality of a member state is therefore a member of the European Union, and as a result you have the freedom to live and or travel anywhere in the EU.

For those dreaming of starting a business in Italy or the EU, being a citizen makes the process easier, but not painless.

There is still much red-tape to cut through if you want to buy or open a business in Italy. And, Italy is actively seeking outside investment money right now. As a citizen, the process is far easier than if you are a foreigner.

Here is the web site punch list that I give my clients to see if they qualify: *http://www.italiamerica.org/id71.htm - engjurequa*

If you were born in any country where citizenship was acquired by birth and any of the following situations applies to you may be considered an Italian citizen. Note that for each category all conditions must be met.

Your father was an Italian citizen at the time of your birth and you have never renounced your right to Italian citizenship. Your mother was an Italian citizen at the time of your birth, AND you were born after January 1, 1948 AND you never renounced your right to Italian citizenship.

Your father was born here in the United States AND your grandfather was an Italian citizen at the time of his birth AND neither you nor your father ever renounced your right to Italian citizenship.

Your mother was born in the United States, AND your mother's mother was an Italian citizen at the time of your birth, AND you were born after January 1, 1948 AND neither you nor your mother ever renounced your right as an Italian citizen. Right to Italian citizenship.

Your paternal or maternal grandfather was born in the United States; your paternal great grandfather was an Italian citizen at the time if his birth, neither you nor your father nor your grandfather ever renounced you right to Italian citizenship.

Additional Information That You Might Find Helpful:

A. A woman born before January 1, 1948 can claim Italian citizenship ONLY from her father AND can transfer it to descendants after January I, 1948

B. "Italian citizen at the time of birth" means that he/she did not acquire any other citizenship through naturalization BEFORE the descendants' birth

C. Ancestors naturalized before July 1, 1912 cannot transmit citizenship.

I suggest that the process can be a fun and rewarding one as you gather up documents etc. Make sure that you check with the local Italian Consulate as you gather up the documents and make sure that everything is in apple-pie order.

Whether you decide to become an Italian citizen or not, the process of tracking down documents and stitching together your family history is a rich and rewarding one. As we get older, it seems that these sorts of things become more and more important. I know that was the case with me…for sure!

You will be happy once the process is completed! Believe me!

Chapter Eight

Humor

1. The Sicilian Pin Cushion

I am still taking those damn quills out of my neck. Why? You may ask? Well, it is because I am a complete dork.

Here is the story of the Sicilian Pin Cushion.

Every day I walk along the *Lungomare*, that fantastic portion of ocean shore road that stretches from the Norman Castle in Acicastello to Ognina and on to Catania. The entire *Lungomare* is actually quite long, seven or eight miles at least, but I walk only about half of it, about three miles, each way up and down from the castle. For an old guy like me it is quite a nice way to get the blood flowing every day. The entire walk takes about one hour and a half to do and it really sets the tone of the day for me.

I learned long ago that I must walk no later than 10am in the morning, because if I got caught walking during the high noon hour, the sun would really get to me.

So, with my trusty bottle of water, my iPod, my New Balance walking shoes, my blue T-shirt that says BOSTON proudly on the front, and my DETROIT POLICE baseball cap that a Detroit police officer once traded me for (I gave him a Red Sox hat), I cut a dashing figure indeed as I saunter up and down the *Lungomare* every morning.

Oh yes, did I tell you that lots of pretty young women jog and walk along the *Lungomare* every morning too?

Yup.

Of course, many handsome Sicilian men also jog and walk too, but the bouncing and jouncing Sicilian women are what really inspire me to jump out of bed each day.

I am duly motivated to look good, act suave and debonair, and try not to look too foolish, which did not go as planned on this particular day.

So, I loaded up my iPod with precisely the exact tunes I wanted to listen to. As I recall, there were nineteen tunes from the Gypsy Kings followed by twelve tunes by Bob Marley. They were perfect summer walking tunes, in my opinion.

After I adjusted my cap and turned the music on, I started to walk at a brisk pace, following behind two women in their mid to late thirties. One of the women was named Giovanna, a striking redhead who I once actually approached and struck up a conversation. The other was her lovely walking companion Maura, a dark-haired beauty and a Sicilian treasure.

I loved it when such a fortuitous event such as this occurred because every once and a while they actually acknowledge me and smile right at me, which would really make my day.

On this day they were really walking as a fast clip, faster that I usually walk. But, being duly inspired and all, I was determined to keep up with these lovely ladies at all cost. Turning up the volume to one particularly lively Gypsy Kings tune, I bounced along the *Lungomare* and was a steady twelve paces behind the ladies, really enjoying my walk.

The miles flew by. Sweat was dripping from my face and my T-shirt was soaked, but still I kept pace.

Just as the last Gypsy Kings finished, I glanced at my iPod to switch to Bob Marley, when all of a sudden…

THWACK!

I had walked into a Fico d'India branch that was hanging over the road. Do you know what a Fico d'India tree is? A cactus. In America, it is called a cactus pear or prickly pears. Guess what? They don't call them prickly pears for nothing!

I had stupidly walked into a low-hanging cactus branch! I had not been paying attention to what I was doing as I had looked down to adjust the iPod and THWACK! Right into it!

Now I had cactus needles stuck into my neck, my shoulder and my arm…a lot of them...and they hurt like hell!

I must have yelped in pain or something as the branch assaulted me, because my groaning had caused my two Sicilian beauties to turn to see what the commotion was all about.

Seeing me now looking like a pin cushion, both women placed their hands over their mouths to stifle laughter…then raced to my aid.

I had never been struck with cactus needles before and now I had at least a hundred needles sticking in me. And I was trying to pull them out …one by one!

Suddenly, my two Sicilian heroines raced to my rescue and began helping me pull the needles out of my neck and shoulder.

Now, let me tell you something, I know an opportunity when I see one. When the needles pinched a little and were a little painful I milked it for all it was worth.

There I was, on a sidewalk in Acicastello, looking like a pin cushion with all these little cactus needles sticking all over the place, and two gorgeous Sicilian women lovingly coming to my rescue and pulling them out.

In any case, tonight I have a dinner date with both of them. The "rescued" thanking his "rescuers."

Smile.

I think I will limp a bit too tomorrow on my walk, maybe even trip and fall in front of another two women.

You never know. On second thought, being a Sicilian pin cushion wasn't such a bad thing after all!

2. The Cappiduzzu

I just love the "Cappidduzzu"…you know what I am talking about, right?

The Cappidduzzu is THE hat worn by anyone who is anyone in Sicily and in Italy, that's what. To not have a cappidduzzu in the winter….why you just as mind as well walk around naked!

All my life I have worn one starting in early fall each year and finially putting it away in late spring….begrudgingly. Not only do I wear one…but so do my son…and my grandson…and I hope that for many generations down the line many of my progeny follow in this path.

The cappidduzzu you see is a sacred implement for the body as well as the soul.

I have had many over the course of my life, but I need to tell you about two of them.

You should know, however, that in my previous life, I was not skilled in the art of properly selecting a cappidduzzu. Mostly, if it fit on my head and the price was right, I would buy it.

I used to envision myself as a young Robert DeNiro back in those days and I always wore my hat exactly like he did ...kinda tilted down over my eyes....Gosh...I was so cool back then.

As I got older and became wise to the ways of dressing for public presentation, know here as "bella figura", I learned that the color of the cappidduzzu should roughly match the color of the outer garment worn. Thus, over time, my cappidduzzu collection grew to match my fall and winter wear.

Grey, black and dark brown cappidduzzu were a stock item of mine well since...forever it seems.

The reason that I wore a cappidduzzu back then is exactly the same reason that I wear it today: I remember my grandfathers.

When I was a little tyke, I have vivid memories about visiting each of them each of them on a cold winter's day and that they would lift me on their knee and let me have a teaspoon or two of coffee and anisette.

Thus, I spent half my childhood in the bag, I guess, but I had a good time!

For some reason, coffee, anisette, and a cappidduzzu still put me in a serene and peaceful place filled with many beautiful memories.

My favorite color of all was dark grey. I found that if the shade was a good enough shade of dark grey, you could get away wearing it with that black leather coat or that brown leather jacket or any coat for that matter if you were too lazy to look for the other matching hats.

Over time, cappidduzzu molds perfectly around the head too, combining comfort and completing the persona.

I just love my cappidduzzu.

About ten years ago, while in Rome, I bought my first "dress" cappidduzzu. You never heard of a dress cappidduzzu? Well, believe me...they have them!

For one hundred and twenty five euro (gulp)...about one hundred and fifty dollars... I bought my first Borsalino cappidduzzu. Borsalino hats are the Mercedes of the cappidduzzu world.

I remember that when I first slipped it on my head that I had an out of body experience. Geez, I had never experienced cashmere on my head before. Prior to this treasure sitting handsomely on my head, only cheap one hundred percent wool hats had sat atop my "testa". I had arrived in life, I thought.

The hat was so beautiful that for the past ten years, I have worn it maybe one or two times.

This hat is now exactly like my nana's living room furniture was… so expensive that she never took the plastic coverings off, and we were never allowed to sit on them. Thus, I feel the same way about my hat.

I would never forgive myself if I lost it or dirtied it or ruined this beauty, so as a result, it stands stoically on my hat shelf getting passed over time and again as I reach for a hat.

Yes…I must admit, I still prefer the wool cappidduzzu. The proletariat of hats. If I get one dirty or get one wet…so what? Isn't that what hats are supposed to be for?

Last year I did suffer a trauma of sorts though. I had this other favorite hat that I had purchased for sixty five euro at a hat shop in Catania. It was a blend of wool and cashmere. Over time, this hat and I were inseparable. For every one hundred times I would wear a hat, ninety five times I would reach for this one.

In any case, one day last winter I was at my sister's house for Sunday dinner, and as I got there she took my jacket and coat. After a wonderful meal and many hours had passed, it was time to leave, but when she got my coat…there was no hat.

After tearing the place apart I left…distraught that my favorite hat was now missing in action.

I remember placing calls to my sister for days afterward asking if she had found the hat yet…to the point that she probably thought I had a hat fetish or something.

To make a long story short, earlier this spring she called me and told me what really had happened to that hat. Evidently it accidently got mixed up with the linen from that Sunday's dinner and was washed with the linen…in the washing machine.

The result was that my cappidduzzu was now a beanie. It had shrunk to the size of a child's hat!

Well, this week I rectified the problem.

This week, I went back to Catania and purchased a hand made, dark grey Barbisio cappidduzzu for ninety euro and am now in therapy to learn how to wear it.

This beauty will not sit on a shelf.

No...I will wear proudly this 100% cashmere treasure everywhere I go this winter...except one place that is.

When I go to my sister's house for dinner, I will wear my baseball hat instead!

3. The Juggler and the Dolt

I food shop at A&O Supermarket which is a great market located on the hill in Aci Catena, close to my condo.

It is a great place that has everything I need and I can in and out of there in two seconds.

The people who work there know me and always give me a big greeting. The check out gal Maria is a cutie pie and I always flirt with her...here big brown eyes and that big smile of hers usually sends me...and all the male customers for that matter...into orbit.

I always go into her line...for sure.

Carmelo, on the other hand, is the male check-out person. He is a character. He takes the mundane job of checking out things at the cash register and makes them fun and the customer's really enjoy watching him operate.

He stands and waits on the customers when he checks them out and does not sit in a chair at the register like all the other cashiers do in Sicily. He is almost American in that way. He greets each customer like they are his long lost brother or sister and he really puts on a show as he rings in all the items that the customers put on the conveyor belt.

Do you remember the movie that Tom Cruise starred in years ago about the bartender? In that movie, Tom Cruise played a very cool and handsome character that all the women went crazy about because he would flip the bottles of alcohol in the air, twirl the bottles in his hand, flip them behind his back and generally make a command performance for them while mixing their drinks.

Later of course, he would conquer them.

Carmelo is the supermarket version of Tom the bartender.

He does the same thing, except he uses the groceries that the customers buy as his props.

He twirls the grocery items in the air, tosses them behind his back, catches them, and flips them…while never dropping a single item. He really puts on a show like I have never seen before.

All to get the attention of the women…and with his striking good looks, it is a snap for him too, I bet.

As a result, he is a very popular check out guy, and the women usually are in his line, and the guys usually are in Maria's line.

One day last week, instead of going through Maria's line to gawk at her, I decided to go through Carmelo's line. I wanted to see if I could do what Carmelo does.

As he rang my stuff through the register…a can of tuna, coffee, fish, cheese, a bottle of olive oil, honey…he flipped each behind his back and caught each one of them…much to the delight of the customers behind me.

Several even clapped.

Now at this point in the story I need to tell you that in Sicily, as opposed to the stores in America, it is the customer, not the clerk who bags the grocery items. So, the clerk rings up the goods, and the customer is the one that puts them either in a bag that he brings with him from home (re-cycling is now the rage in Sicily) or the customer is charged fifteen cents for a skimpy plastic bag (this is what always happens to me …I always forget to bring a nice cloth bag that I have from home).

On this particular day, as usual, I forgot my bag, and had to buy a plastic one.

As Carmelo was ringing in my first item, a can of tuna, he flipped it behind his back and then handed it to me.

Wanting to impress Carmelo and also the ten other folks watching the show, I in turn flipped the can behind my back and stuck it into my bag.

The customers cheered me.

He did the same with the coffee…flipping it in the air, catching it, ringing it up and then throwing it to me. I caught the can of coffee, flipped it up in the air, and dropped it deftly into the bag too.

The crowd was delighted. They roared.

We continued our performance. He twirled and did a one-handed catch with the grapes…so did I.

He did a reverse toss over his shoulder with the strawberry jam and I reacted with precision accordingly.

We were two maestros perfectly in sync that day. Like two artists painting the exact same picture at the same time.

We were, as Mr. Minyagi said in The Karate Kid…in perfect harmony with each other.

That is…until he tossed me the bottle of olive oil.

Yup…you guessed it. I caught it and tossed it high into the air…. and in slow motion it came down…I thought into the bag…but instead it landed on the counter…I had misjudged the velocity of the bottle as it came down…and SPLAT…

All over the place!

One liter of one hundred percent first press extra virgin olive oil…came crashing down on the check out counter and exploded everywhere.

I could not believe how much oil was really in that bottle! Enough to re-float the Titanic… and now it was seeping everywhere!

Since flipping grocery items is a precision science and art…almost like those airplane air shows that we see on the television…the noise from the exploding oil bottle momentarily distracted Carmelo and as a result, my half liter bottle of the finest Sicilian honey that you could ever find…slipped from his hands behind him …and fell to the floor… and also exploded into a gooey mess!

Oh my God! What a mess! What embarrassment! What humiliation! I shrunk to two inches tall in two seconds!

Between the oil seeping all over the place and the honey oozing everywhere, our command performance had turned into a stinker of a performance in a matter of seconds.

Of course everyone burst into laughter. It was a hilarious sight… me covered with oil and Carmelo's pants covered with honey and the whole area now a disaster zone.

Naturally, it was the woman who came to the rescue.

Lovely Maria bolted from her station at her register and immediately swung into action, and within a matter of minutes the only thing that was still noticeable was our bruised egos.

Carmelo was a little bit sheepish, but nothing keeps that guy down for long.

The show must go on as they say!

Within five minutes, he was back to flipping things in the air again, but I learned my lesson.

I was done, *finito* with show business. From now on, I will stick to Maria's line and just gawk at the woman who rescued us from complete embarrassment that day!

Tonight I think I will watch that Tom Cruise film again…I must have missed something; maybe he can teach me a few more pointers…

Then again, maybe he can't!

4. True Confession (Maybe)

The confession that you are about to read may or may not be completely true. The names have been changed to protect the innocent:

Sinner: Bless me father, for I have sinned. This is my first time at confession in Sicily, so I may be a little off here.

Priest: That is all right, my son. Most of us here are a little off here. Where are you from?

Sinner: I am from the United States. I live in Acitrezza now.

Priests: Did you go to confession in the states?

Sinner: I used to but then all the priests got thrown in jail.

Priest: That's been a problem lately. What can I do for you?

Sinner: I think I committed heresy, but I am not sure.

Priest: Do you mean that you spoke against our Lord and Savior Jesus Christ, my child?

Sinner: Oh no. Not that. I made pasta sauce and I used ketchup instead of tomatoes.

Priest: Wha…

Sinner: I had some people coming over for dinner last night from Taormina and I had only one small can of crushed tomatoes. I figured that if I used plenty of oil, garlic, red pepper flakes, salt, pepper and fresh garlic, I could get away with it.

Priest. Why did you think that?

Sinner: They were from Taormina.

Priest: I see. Did you?

Sinner: Of course. I said they were from Taormina. They always think everything is better there anyway, so I had nothing to lose.

Priest: I see. OK. Since there is a little truth to that, the Lord forgives you. Did they eat the pasta?

Sinner: Of course. They are from Taormina and it was free.

Priest: I see. You are correct, of course. Have you done anything else bad, my son?

Sinner: Yes.

Priest: And what is that my son?

Sinner: I eat regularly at MacDonald's in Acireale.

Priest: What? You eat regularly there? No one eats regularly there, my son! The only people who go there are parents who take their kids there for a Happy Meal party on their birthdays. What is wrong with you, my son?

Sinner: I never had wine with a Big Mac before, father. It's pretty good. It really hides the taste.

Priest: You mean to tell me that in the United States they do not offer wine at MacDonald's?

Sinner: Yes, father. No wine.

Priest: Now that's heresy!

Sinner: Thank you so much, father. Plus, the espresso and cornetti is free between 8:00 am and 10:00 am every day. I cannot help myself. I disguise myself, slip in for *pranzo*, wolf down a burger or two, and feel guilty all day long.

Priest: This is a terrible burden you carry. You are forgiven, my son. Anything else? We are getting kinda backed up with the line. People must think I have Satan in here.

Sinner: No, father, that is about it. Thank you for listening to me. I feel a lot better.

Father: Well, say a few Hail Mary's and a couple Our Fathers and we'll call it even, OK? I have one last question though.

Sinner: Sure, father, what is it?

Priest: I have some people coming over from Siracusa tonight. What brand did you say that ketchup was? They love free stuff too. Think they will know?

Sinner: I think you will be all set, father. They are from Siracusa plus it’s free!

Priest: You are correct, of course…go in peace, my son…

Chapter Nine

Home Away From Home

Here I am in my sixties, waiting on tables in Sicily.

How did this happen?

Well, I'm not really waiting tables.

It is not that I get paid or anything. I do it out of love. I do it for my Sicilian family. They aren't really my family in the true definition, but I think of them as family just the same.

Meet my brother Roberto, sisters Nancy, Maria-Grazia, Sonja, and, of course …mamma.

Then, there is also Saro, Salvo, and Christian who are all employees of the family but are in reality are treated like family members. There are also various and sundry friends, bon vivants, and locals who are everyday fixtures at the home of the family.

Welcome to Café Sikelia, the home of the family. It is located in the Recanati section of Giardini Naxos.

It is the best place in Naxos. It is a popular café, bar, restaurant, gathering place, and nerve center in this part of the island. Café Sikelia is my home away from home.

This is my story - of how I became involved with these wonderful people. It is their story too.

I stumbled into Café Sikelia back in 1999, when I was on holiday in Sicily with I do not remember who to be honest with you. In those days, my life was a blur, a revolving door of friends, women and travel companions.

I had found Sicily and fell in love with her. Café Sikelia would be the testament to that love.

Roberto cut a dashing figure back then. (Actually, he still does today.) Tall, dark, handsome, cultured, smart, funny, multi-lingual, he is the co-owner, along with his sister Sonja, of the Café. He is the major personality of the Café.

He waits tables, engages in conversation with people from all walks of life on virtually any subject, and is really an entertainer of sorts. People come to Café Sikelia for Roberto, not just for the food or drink, both of which are excellent. They also came for the ambiance and laid back atmosphere.

Here you can have a great meal and spend the night just enjoying yourself.

While Roberto is the star of the show, the supporting cast is wonderful as well.

First, there is Sonja, the fabulous and beautiful sister and business partner of Roberto, who co-owns the Café with Roberto and puts in just as many hours per week (who knows how many...countless) as he does.

Tall, dark-haired, and elegant, she is the perfect Sicilian beauty; she is one thousand percent Sicilian.

Ah, to be twenty years younger, I often say to her!

Roberto is the schmoozer; she is the brains behind the operation. She speaks only halting English, but communicates well enough with the clients to get by. She is a tried and true professional and a testament to the modern Sicilian woman.

Then there is Maria-Grazia who speaks English very well and lives in Holland six months a year with her fiancée. This stunning woman is cultured, refined, elegant and generous. I cannot walk into that place without Maria insisting that I eat something. She helps out in the morning and for the busy lunch and dinner hours, and also does the paperwork and errands too. For the busy tourist season, she comes home from Holland to help the family out, and she puts in just as many hours as Roberto and Sonja.

Then there is Nancy who runs the gift shop and clothing store down the street named after their mother, Ida. Nancy is also a businesswoman with elegant taste in clothes. All throughout Naxos the locals wear what she buys at the high fashion shows in Milan every year. Casual and elegant clothes, shoes, bags and the like are on sale at Ida's boutique. It is a very nice place and is the place in Naxos to shop.

Thus, the four siblings were the exception in Sicily as far as I could see. Four workaholics, driven to succeed and they were certainly doing it. They were Sicilian but had adopted the American work ethic.

This was, of course, because of mamma, the strong mother of the four siblings who held court every day at both locations. During the day she could be found at the boutique and at nighttime she would be in a back table at the café holding court with friends, and subtly giving direction and guidance. She had skimped and saved all her money when she was younger and invested it in property and businesses in Naxos, a little at a time. Now, her four children had opportunity in life.

She still has much to teach them about the ways of business. The four children are sponges, absorbing all her comments and directives.

Café Sikelia is located exactly across the street from the Hilton-Naxos, the biggest hotel and conference center around.

Vacationers and business people come from all over the world to vacation here, to meet and hold conventions. Tour operators have firsthand experience with how good the Café is because their clients tell them how much they loved Sikelia.

Tour operators send group after group there for various welcoming dinners, cooking demonstrations, wine tasting, and just about every other activity created by Roberto.

Back in 1999, when I first went there, I admired Roberto from afar as I marveled at his business acumen. As I continued to frequent the place, we became friends.

Then we became fast friends.

Then we became best friends.

Then we became brothers.

That is the way it is when two personalities connect. However, the same occurred with me and Sonja, Maria-Grazia, Nancy, and mamma too. They became my second family in no time.

Café Sikelia was seared into my heart and soul in the year 2000.

In October of that year, as I will explain in a chapter in just a few pages, and while on holiday with my son Matt, I met a woman from Amsterdam at the Café who I later married. Thus, the Café holds significance for me.

Over the years, the Café has become my refuge in Sicily where I go to heal myself from this trauma or that trauma. This is the place I go to heal myself emotionally time and time again. It is the place where I have experienced some of the happiest moments of my life.

I continued to return to Sikelia for many years…first as a client, then as a friend...then as a brother, and finally as a family member. Somewhere along the line, Roberto stopped giving me a bill and because I am not a moocher, I started helping the family.

This is why I wait on tables.

Until I became a personality of sorts myself.

Café Sikelia had become a popular spot with a few tour operators in Europe and especially with one large tour operator in America.

While Roberto speaks English well enough to charm the socks off of all the Americans who take part in his welcome dinners as they arrive into Naxos. Welcome dinners are special dinners arranged by each tour operator for their clients on the first night of their arival in Sicily. I found myself hosting these dinners along with Roberto.

Roberto would offer to his clients a wonderful dinner in a cordial and friendly atmosphere. This was very important to Roberto because during the week, the diners might return and they might in turn recommend Cake Sikelia to friends on the various tourists' blogs.

Roberto, Sonja and the staff took these dinners very seriously, and offered great food, wonderful hospitality and a great atmosphere. Even a wandering Sicilian troupe would come in to sing authentic Sicilian songs after dinner.

The offerings of soups, Sicilian appetizers, and main courses were delicious, plentiful, and most importantly, were offered at a special price to each tour operator that wouldn't break the bank.

These dinners were a win-win for everyone. The tour operators loved them because the clients later raved about them, and the dinners offered a steady stream of clients into Café Sikelia.

That is where I came in.

I noticed that Roberto often times had thirty-five to forty American clients at once in the Café. This presented a problem sometimes, as he was the only English-speaker on the staff if Maria-Grazie was helping in other areas.

I began to pitch in, and help the clients, first explaining the menu's offerings to them, then pouring an endless supply of wine, then clearing the tables and finally schmoozing with the clients the way that a Sicilian like me, who has kissed the Sicilian Blarney Stone, can do!

I frequently engaged in conversations with clients about all sorts of topics ranging from the history of Sicily, to my favorite spots here to the political climate in Europe and just about every other topic you could think of pertaining to Sicily and the European Union.

Roberto would tell me that I was great. He told me that the clients loved me and that I was the reason that they would come back the next day for lunch or dinner.

I had inadvertently become a mini-tourist attraction myself!

This was especially so because I had thrown a bunch of my first two books into my suitcase as I had left America and these clients were starting to buy autographed copies. I sold more and more every day. To me this was a great way for me to introduce The Sicilian Project to people. The Sicilian Project is my pet project where we are teaching English to Sicilian students paid for by American donations that I solicit. Thus, I was happy to help out!

I was helping Roberto, engaging is pleasant talk with many interesting and wonderful people, promoting Sicily, promoting the Cafe, helping Roberto and the family, and now selling books and getting donations for the Sicilian Project too!

Here I was, a sixty year old recovering from a cardiac issue from the previous year, working as a schmoozer and a waiter in a Café in Sicily 5400 kilometers from my hometown in Lawrence, Massachusetts. I loved every minute of it.

What a life!

The best thing of all, however, is that my "second" family…my Sicilian family…is in my heart and is now a part of who I am.

What more can a man ask for?

Nothing, really…if you think about it. I am blessed, and I know it.

Chapter Ten

Road Trip with "Only" Vita - Part One

A Healing Journey

Just my luck to find a woman that I have a lot in common with and could really be happy with except for two things: (1) She didn't comply with the Jennifer Rule and (2) She didn't feel remotely the same way that I did about her. She felt something, but I never figured out exactly what it was.

Probably sorrow for me. Who knows?

In any case, here is the story about "only" Vita and I think it a fascinating one. I will take her memory to my grave, for sure. I think that you will like our adventures.

In June of this year, I was spending a lot of time in Naxos at Roberto's place Café Sikelia. I set up shop in the back of the Café and held court there with all sorts of different people. When the

American tour groups came once a week, I was the official host, translator, and schmoozer. I loved it, plus I sold a ton of my books. So, there was a reason I was doing it. It was good for me, and good for my pocketbook, which was currently full of lint.

Café Sikelia has held a special place in my heart for a long time and for a lot of reasons. As this story unfolds you will understand why. In any case, and as is my habit, Roberto's' place has always been my base of operations.

Roberto's' place is also a magnet for those in the travel business, especially for travel guides from all over to meet, relax, chit chat and to plan events for their clients.

Five weeks ago, as I walked into Café Sikelia, I saw Vita.

I do not know what struck me first about her; was it her stunning blue eyes? Was it that sultry Baltic look she had? Was it that lithe, exquisite athletic body? Was it that "stays away from me, mister" look that she had? What was it? A scent? I hadn't a clue. It was something, though…that I knew.

I knew immediately that I was attracted to her on some level, and I quickly concluded that I wanted to get to know her better…a lot better. I decided to investigate and to see who this lovely woman was. Usually, when I decide to get to know someone, I am ruthlessly efficient. Years of an Alpha Wolf existence had taught me to be very proficient. As I would later find out, this so-called training of mine turned out to be completely useless with Vita.

Simply stated: Vita could not and cannot be labeled or typecast. She is a unique soul…but at the time, I hadn't a clue.

I did ask Roberto about her. Who is she, I asked? I found out that her name was Vita and that she worked for a tour company as a guide, and that she was Lithuanian but had lived all over - Greece, Spain, and Northern Italy.

I found out also that she spoke several languages, English and Russian being two of them. I found out that she had the reputation of being one of the best guides out there, and I found out that she was in her mid to late thirties.

Obviously, I found out she was single too.

"As long as she passes the Jennifer Rule", I thought to myself, "no problem. I'll take a shot at her".

Right. The Jennifer Rule. That rule is sometimes bane of my existence.

The Jennifer Rule was an agreement that I had negotiated years ago with my eldest daughter

Jennifer. I call her *Jennifer the Wise*. Simply stated, I had agreed that I would date no women that were younger than *Jennifer the Wise*. I had kept this agreement pretty much true and fast since I had separated four years previously from my Russian wife.

While I had flirted in the past with women near Jennifer's age, Vita looked like she might be right on the cusp. This would be a close call, I thought.

Well, to make a long story short, it was apparent from the beginning that Vita had no interest in me romantically. None whatsoever. Being suave, debonair and refined would not work with her. She was way past that.

As a matter of fact, I quickly found out that she was one of the most spiritually perfect creatures I was to ever meet, and not only that, material possessions meant little or nothing to her. At this nascent stage, I knew nothing about any of that stuff. Not that it mattered to me. I had never let another's feelings for me in the past be dispositive of my actions, and this was the case here.

I was, after all, an Alpha Dog, and a proficient one at that. Well, in my head, at least.

I was immediately smitten with this woman for some reason and I knew it and I wanted to be sure that she knew it. And, I telegraphed it this to her. I didn't care whether she knew it or not. It was what it was.

As a matter of fact, within a couple minutes of meeting her, I told her that.

"Hello, my name is Alfred." I said. "Would you like to marry me?" I asked.

Smiling at me with those haunting blue eye of hers, she said "The computer says no, Alfred, but I think I might like you as a friend. But do not think anything else. I will like you in a friendly way."

"My name is only Vita." She said.

In any case, I found out that she was in fact a few months younger that Jennifer, so for reasons one and two cited above, my love for *only Vita* was doomed right from the start.

For you see, *only Vita* came into my life on this day for a reason, and the trips that we were about to take together all over Sicily for a five month period would prove to be a healing series of journeys for me… something that someone once said happens only once in a lifetime.

I had just met *only Vita* and she was about to rock my world. Except at this time, I did not know it.

I have concluded now that these trips were good for Vita too, but I do not speak for her, and that is getting ahead of myself.

At the time I met her, I did not understand what was about to happen to me on these journeys. Now I fully understand them.

Vita, as I later surmised, was sent to me for a reason from a greater power, and I really believe now that I was sent to her too for a reason.

I do not think that we now have a normal friendly friendship. I think we have a type of friendship now that is undefined. "Deep and true" and perhaps "forever" and perhaps "temporary" are only words and I am still struggling to find the appropriate ones that fit here, to be honest with you.

I do know, however, and I told this to her, that this she is forever etched in my heart and my memory in a powerful and loving way, and I do not care what definition that she or anyone else uses for that word. This woman, completely unintentionally and with no apparent reason that I can articulate…would rocked my world and became my Beatrice. She became my inspiration. Dante had Beatrice, I was about to have *only Vita*.

But that is getting ahead of myself, isn't it? Let us proceed with this tale.

Within a matter of days we started hanging out a bit here, and a bit there. I would be at Roberto's and she would walk in; she would be at Roberto's and I would walk in. She would meet clients there. The point is, we kept bumping into each other.

We would have coffee, talk, hang at the Café. We killed time. I think she found my brash American demeanor odd and probably offensive. Most of the time, I am offensive in a brash sort of way. Baltic men are reserved. I am the complete opposite. I am an offensively offensive and unreserved. I am the anti-Baltic man. But I am comfortable in my skin.

I think she found me intelligent. I think she was attracted, on the surface, to my intelligence. Plus, I made her laugh a lot too.

In any case, out of the blue, I invited her to take a two day road trip with me.

It was a "flyer" as we called it in the states. Ask a question that you know almost with certainty the answer to, but hope for a different one.

I wanted to see Piazza Armerina in Casale, Gela, Agrigento and Sciacca and a bunch of small towns in-between as research for this book, and thought to myself that the worst she could say was no.

To my surprise, she texted me the next day and told me that she had two days free, and why not.

She would come with me in a "friendly way", meaning exactly that. Don't try anything, bucko.

I quickly agreed. Honestly, I just wanted to be with her at this point...I just had to. Why, I do not know. Something was calling me, and I was a little afraid to find out what.

Thus started an odyssey thru the center of Sicily and continuing south and west into the innards of many small Sicilian coastal towns accompanied by perhaps the most magnificent human being that I had met in years.

Unknown to me at the time, I was starting a journey of discovery, a journey of healing, a most remarkable gift that was about to be given to me by a most remarkable person and for a remarkable unknown reason.

This wasn't just going to be just a road trip for cultural reasons I was beginning to believe.

No…something special was going to happen to me.

The heck with the road trip, I thought, I am going to spend time with *only Vita* and see where this goes and even though she looked at me only in one way, in a friendly way, I did not care one whit.

This was way beyond that stuff, honestly.

Something was about to happen to me, heck, it was already happening… something cleansing, and something spiritual and something that I needed to find an answer to...quickly.

From the moment I read her text that she would come with me, my world went off kilter.

Before I can continue the story of Vita though, and the first road trip, I need to introduce you to a person that I have buried in the recesses of my mind and spirit for a long time.

To understand about what happened on this most remarkable adventures with *only Vita* that unfolded over a five month period, I now have to introduce you to Leonie …the true love of my life.

Once I introduce you to her, you will begin to understand.

Leonie

These words are really hard to write. They have been buried in the deepest of the deepest recesses of my heart for over a decade. The memories have been chained in a box deep in my heart, hidden from all.

Last year, the lock was slightly jarred when I met other women named Gabriella who gave it a ping, enough to let me know that something was still there.

Vita, however, would unlocked the box - not purposely, mind you, but the box was ready to be unlocked. She inadvertently unlocked it.

Now, the ghost was unleashed, and it had to be buried.

I met Leonie in October of 2000 in Naxos, at Roberto's Cafe Sikelia while there with my son Matt on a father-son holiday and in she walked one day with her sister.

She was Dutch, from Holland and on holiday. She was beautiful; knock your socks off beautiful.

She was blond, haunting hazel eyes, Romanesque figure, lithe and young. From the entrance of Café Sikelia when Leonie entered to where I was sitting was no more than twenty feet.

How long does it take to walk twenty feet? Five or ten seconds? Well, if that is the case that is how long it took me to fall hopelessly in love with this woman. She entered Roberto's' place, our eyes locked briefly, I fell in love. That simple. Bang. Just like that. I fell off the ledge. I fell in love.

After a long life with many women along the way, for the first time, the Alpha Dog was silenced. I became a puppy in a nano-second. I did not even know this woman's name.

She and her sister sat at the table next to me. I was so excited that I think I had heart palpitations.

My mouth went dry. For the first time in my life, I struggled with words.

We talked. The words stumbled out of my mouth, but we talked. For three hours. We talked, and I never asked her name. Finally, at 3am in the morning, she told me that she had to go because she and her sisters were leaving for Holland the next morning early and they had to pack. Saying good bye, they left.

Just like that. They left. I had no name, no number, no address, no anything.

Not knowing what hit me, I knew that I had to do SOMETHING, and do it quick.

I knew the name of the hotel they were staying as it was right next to the one I was staying. That was a start. I walked into that hotel and the night clerk asked what I wanted. I told him that I wanted to speak to the beautiful Dutch girl who just walked in.

After pocketing a twenty euro tip, he called her, and to my surprise, she came down.

I asked her name. She told me: Leonie. I told her that I was sorry to bother her, but I had come to tell her that when I had seen her for the first time, something happened to me, and that I was probably being foolish saying that, but I had to tell her. I told her that I was sorry to bother her, I said, but I had to tell her that to her face before she disappeared into the wind forever.

As I turned to walk away, she said to me "I felt the same way, Alfred."

I froze in my tracks as I recall hearing those words.

She left the next day, but we met the next weekend in London. We met the following weekend after that weekend in London too. We stayed at the Chesterfield in the Mayfair district. We were like two teenagers. We feel deeply in love. Eternally in love. Forever in love. Our molecules intermingled.

We became one. Dante wrote about this type of love. I was experiencing it. He was so very right. I love that guy Dante.

By the third week, when I went to Amsterdam for the first time, we were making plans to marry.

After a seven month whirlwind romance, we married, and we had parties both in America and in Holland. *Jennifer the Wise* and Matt came to Holland to celebrate a magical time there. We set up a small apartment in Holland and like two lovebirds, we were happy.

My condo in Massachusetts became a home instantly when she crossed that threshold. I cannot adequately describe the feelings I was experiencing, but I was on the highest of highs, the kind writers spend careers writing unsuccessfully about…and here I am…on top of the mountain yelling it out loud for all to see and hear.

Here I was, at age 50, hopelessly in love with a magnificent creature, and she, at age 37 had also met her soul mate. I completed her she would tell me. "We will grow old, sit on a bench by the canal and hold hands" she would tell me.

This lasted until January 5, 2002. Fourteen months.

I remember the date because we had spent the holidays in Amsterdam and I had to return to the states for a client. She wanted to stay a few extra days to be with her parents, and I said OK.

While I was on the plane coming back to America……BAM….

She suffered three devastating brain aneurysms.

I remember getting my luggage at Logan airport in Boston and going outside and turning on my cell phone. There was a message from Yaap, the boyfriend of Caroline, Leonie's sister.

He told me that she had suffered three brain aneurysms, and that the surgery she had been unsuccessful, and that I better get back to Amsterdam fast. She probably wasn't going to make it.

Imagine hearing those words…out of the blue…about a woman that you desperately loved…and had made passionate love with only a few hours earlier?

My spirit died instantly. I reeled and almost fainted. My knees buckled that day at Logan.

Unknown to me, hearing those words, I later found out, I had suffered a silent heart attack, but at the time all I knew is that I had to get back to Holland fast because my wife was dying.

I caught the next plane out of Logan, and for six months I was at Leonie's side at the University of Leiden Medical Center in Leiden Holland, looking at her, praying for her, feeling completely helpless.

I was living in Holland, a stranger in a strange land. Living a nightmare. I just could not comprehend how this happened and I was angry…at who I do not know, but I was angry.

In any case, she woke up one day, but the Leonie I knew wasn't there.

After several months, we returned to the states, but by then the handwriting was on the wall: I could not take care of her and she really needed to be in Holland.

My law practice, my kids, my life was in America. I could not just uproot and leave everything behind.

Thus, we divorced reluctantly after two more years. I could not do it, I just could not do it. I felt dirty because I was a failure. I felt that I had violated my vow of "in sickness and in health". It killed me. I had no choice. I could not care for her in America, and I could not make a living in Holland. Her parents and her sisters were a far better support group than I. I faced the facts.

As for my heart? I locked it up and threw away the key.

A couple years later I met and married a lovely Russian woman, but I did not give the relationship a chance. It was destined to failure from the beginning, which it did.

Now you know the story about Leonie.

Thus, sitting at Roberto's' that day and seeing *only Vita* that first time, and feeling the electricity flow through my body like it had done a decade earlier, and realizing that Vita did not feel the same as me (how could she?), I just needed to be with her for a while to process exactly what I was feeling.

I needed closure with Leonie, I guess, and this first trip with Vita was going to be the trip I never got to take with my wife. Vita was going to heal me, and she hadn't a clue about what was about to happen, and neither did I at this point. It just happened.

Well, now that you know this part of the story, I guess I can continue on.

First, though, I have to tape my heart together again, because it still hurts to tell the story, even after all this time.

Day One

The plan was to take back roads everywhere. Anyone in Sicily can get from point A to point B by traveling on a highway someplace. We decided to take a highway only when necessary, which meant that we had a decent map with us in the car.

The plan the first day was to leave from Naxos, and then head south toward Catania, then veer west toward Enna, but pull off the Autostrada just after we hit the Plains of Catania, that vast stretch of stark and open farmland that stands in sharp contrast with any other area in Sicily.

From there we would work our way through the back roads of Sicily, through sleepy little villages like Bivio Jannarello, Stimpato, Guimarra, Raddusa, Morgantina, Aidone and then hit our first real stop, the Piazza Armerina just outside of Casale.

The day was sunny and hot. The Magic Carpet was ready for the trip. With new tires, new battery, new brakes, there is not much else that can wrong with this little egg beater, and I was sure that we would be able to roll anywhere with it.

In the front seat I bought my portable iPod speakers and my iPod which holds 1500 tunes. With a few bottles of water in the back seat and some fruit, we were set on the first part of the journey.

For me, something felt special as soon as I turned the ignition on and the Magic Carpet hummed to life.

It didn't feel like a car anymore. No, it truly felt like a Magic Carpet. Right from the first kilometer of the first day of the trip, an out of body, surreal experience was happening to me.

We were riding on a magic carpet, Vita and I, and everything I was seeing, feeling, talking about, experiencing was going directly to my emotional data bank in my brain. I was a little frightened, truth be told, because I had never had this type of feeling before.

Vita was, well, Vita. She speaks English, but it is a very different type of English that native English speakers speak. I call it "cute" English. Usually syntax, pronunciation, verb tense, and a lot of things are thrown out the window when talking to one who talks this type of English, but communication was quickly established between the two of us. Actually, as the trip progressed, I found myself talking more like her than vice versa. It was fun actually, to speak "foreign" English if you know what I mean.

I was surprised that Vita liked my choice of music too.

Lately I have been experimenting with all sorts of music, and I really like some of the New Age stuff by Paul Schwartz, Gregorian Chant music, and easy stuff like Bob Marley, Gypsy Kings, Otmar Leibart and a new CD from my pal back in Boston, the lawyer/singer/fantastic person Valerie Giglio who had just released a great CD called *The Italian Project*. That music selection, so very important to my state of mind, somehow perfectly matched the setting for this trip. As it turns out, it played a crucially important part in the whole Vita thing.

The music so perfectly matched the setting that first day that Vita repeatedly asked that a certain song or CD be re-played, and she became especially attached to Valerie's new CD.

As the morning progressed and the Sicilian countryside began to dominate the spirits within both of us, the chit-chat that two people who are getting to know each other engage in gradually stopped, and was replaced by the sights, sounds, colors and textures of the Sicilian countryside as it merged with the haunting music wafting into our ears.

Multiple senses were being simultaneously stimulated; sight, sound, feeling…you name it, things were rapidly getting to a special place.

I do not remember my iPod player sounding so beautiful. Really, I do not.

We stopped here and there to take pictures. One breathtaking vista appeared after another, and we just had to stop. At one point, Vita picked some eucalyptus leaves and rubbed them together for me, just to get the sense of smell involved, I think.

Then we stopped talking, and we began visually communicating with each other.

As the beauty of the countryside unfolded on that brilliant first part of the road trip that morning. Nearly all communication between Vita and I shifted into some form of metaphysical communication caused by the visual beauty of the land and the melding of that beauty with beautiful music. We were two spirits that genuinely were at peace with each other, and getting to like each other too.

Of course, the Alpha Wolf in me could not understand what was happening. No way. The Magic Carpet was now aloft and fully operational. I simply did not understand what was happening to me. The computer did not compute. Not with me, anyway. If it did compute, I was refusing to acknowledge it.

Piazza Armerina and the Roman Villa was more beautiful to experience that any picture book depicts. Really, you must visit this Roman villa that has been lovingly preserved by the Italian authorities. This is really a very special and underrated place. We spent about two hours studying the mosaics of that special place and taking outstanding photos. I noticed that Vita began snapping a few photos of me with her camera. I thought this odd…in a nice sort of way.

Since we were both students of Sicily, we exchanged tidbits of information about the Villa and the surroundings, although this was the first time I had visited the place. Vita had been here before.

We decided to get an espresso before we left the Villa and while we were sitting at the cafe relaxing, my cell phone rang. It was Roberto. He wanted to know how was it was going. Seems like Vita and I were the buzz of Naxos. We both laughed and I passed the cell to her and they chatted. In any case, we continued on to the second phase of the trip for that day.

The plan was to now head south and hit a bunch of small towns on the way to Gela, where we would spend the night. It was about 3pm by this time, and we had another four hours of daylight left we figured. We wanted to be in Gela by sundown because almost none of these back roads have streetlights, and the twists and turns would be particularly difficult at night.

Fiats are known to be dependable cars, especially Puntos, but the headlights are terrible. The lights are weak and unless you drive constantly with the high beams on, you mind as well use a flashlight. Thus, getting to Gela by sundown was imperative.

We headed slightly west and hit the sleepy town of Barrafranca before turning south toward Mazzarino, a beautiful little village resplendent in greenery and villas.

We were in the Sicilian hinterlands now and the scenery took our breathe away time and time again. The visuals were totally different from the coastal towns were I operate usually. Here the land, not the sea, is the centerpiece. I remember distinctly one valley we hit that was so overwhelming with beauty that I commented to Vita that I counted ten different shades of green in one place.

The flamingo guitar in Otmar Liebart's great CD, *Luna Negra*, provided the perfect backdrop for this vista and fused the visuals in my mind.

We passed through countless little villages and towns, most not even listed on the map. Castelluzzo, Butera, San Nicola are but a few... and we stopped many times along the way to admire the beauty of the land, take photos, or just to stop the car and gaze.

The magic carpet ride of this day was perfect as we headed into Gela that evening.

Somehow, I was emotionally drained. I hadn't expected to be emotionally overcome this day, but somehow it had happened. I know that Vita wasn't feeling what I was feeling. How could she? However, she too was now was also on a different plane, and that first day our relationship, while remaining friendly, entered a new phase. We were now special friends. Very special friends.

You have to understand that a generation separates us. She is, after all, younger that *Jennifer the Wise* by five months. Perhaps if the age thing was closer, perhaps if we had met in another life, there are a million perhaps, I guess. What I know is this: I did not want this trip to end.

Something opened in me this day. I did not understand it. And frankly, I did not want to understand it.

We found a hotel, checked in, cleaned up, and had a lovely meal that first night.

By the end of that first day, Vita wasn't just a companion on a road trip. This young woman from Lithuania was my friend. My very good friend. I went to sleep that night and for the first time in twelve years, my heart was at peace.

My soul, my restless soul, relaxed for the first time.

Roberto once told me that with the big round sunglasses that Vita wore all the time that she reminded him of a bumble-bee. I remember smiling at the time and not thinking of it too much.

Then, I realized that those eyes…those big blue eyes…were the gateway to her soul. All it took was a glance at them to see what she was thinking and feeling. And I knew one thing; she was a turtle holding something deep inside her too. Her lips it seemed moved in one direction, but those eyes told a different story. She had a sad story too that she was hiding; she too was protecting her soul. Her eyes told me that.

Gela was rather pedestrian we both agreed. The restaurant that we ate at, supposedly one of the best around was just fair. However, the wine was good, and as the say "in vino veritas", and the conversation that evening, aided by some decent wine and then some decent amaro Averna afterwards, was deep and profound. That is all I will say.

Gela to me seemed like a million other seaside towns that I have seen, even a little on the honky-tonk side. Still, the room was inexpensive and had a great breakfast the following morning. We were refreshed for the next day's adventure, which was going to be a long one.

Day Two

The plan for Day Two was to head to Agrigento and the Valley of the Temples, and then hit Sciacca for a late afternoon lunch, and then start the trek back to Naxos.

All we had to do was keep the sea to our left, and we did what we had done the first day; we found parallel roads that took us thru the Sicilian countryside and avoided the highways as much as possible.

Something was different today though.

A bond had formed between us on the Magic Carpet, and we both very much enjoyed each other's Company albeit in a "friendly way" as Vita kept saying. However, that wasn't what I was saying. I know the chemistry of attraction better than most. I knew also that it had to be reciprocated. I had to be content with a friendship with Vita, and I willingly accepted whatever she gave me.

Truth be told, I was fortunate that I even got that. At this point I was having a hard time. Was this Vita, or was this the spirit of Leonie? Vita was very much her own person, and I now knew and appreciated her very much. Somehow, on the first leg of this trip, the spirit of Leonie was awakened in my soul. I cannot put my finger of when, or why, or how, but something changed in the deepest recesses of my soul. I think it was the fact that I truly enjoyed being part of a special time with a special person. Or maybe it was something else. Maybe my heart was looking for a reason to stop being so restless, maybe it was waiting for a reason. I have no clue. I am terrible reading my feelings and I was confused. All I knew at this point was that this nice gal was somehow healing my soul, in a friendly sort of way.

From Gela, we proceeded west and hit the sleepy but beautiful towns of Manfria, Poggio Lungo and Falconara before arriving at the magnificent and beautiful town of Licata. As we were proficient at doing now, we would hit a village, poke around a bit, take some photos, maybe have a coffee, and move on.

About this time, I asked Vita if I could take a photo of her. She said sure. Thus, I began the process of taking a photo of a beautiful scene, a beautiful mountain, flower, valet, hill, church and then one of Vita too.

Some with her bumble bee sunglasses on, others with them off. Makes no matter. Those images I have saved in a folder now. I know what each tells me. I know what she was thinking when the photo was snapped, and I also know that the eyes never lie. This is what I know.

I told her that someday I will publish a book of the photos of her and call it "Only Vita."

Later, I will explain the significance of the name. Rest assured though that I took some remarkable images of all of the above.

From Licata, we then hugged the coastline and hit all the sea towns between there and Agrigento, Marina di Palma, Cannanello, Akragas, and then finally, Agrigento.

Ancient Agrigento, with the largest collection of Greek ruins - even larger than those of Greece herself, sitting in splendor in the Valley of the Temples. Which, unfortunately, is now a tourist trap with countless tour busses and gift shops everywhere.

We knew this, but we knew a back way into town, and we managed to avoid all that congestion and enjoyed the scenery nonetheless.

Both of us had been here many times, but it was a compulsory stop. Stopping to buy batteries for the camera and the IPOD player and to have an espresso, we ran into four Americans who were lost. They had rented a house up in Nicolosi and had ventured out to see the Greek Temples, but were lost. We chatted for a while. I gave them my card and suggested that if they got to Naxos, they could find me at Café Sikelia. To my surprise, three nights later, the four of them did exactly that and ate a wonderful dinner there. After putting them on the right track, we continued our journey west to Sciacca.

About twenty minutes outside of Agrigento, we took a side trip to the beautiful hill town of Siculiana, once a mafia stronghold whose leadership was wiped out during the Mafia wars and the survivors, the "scappati" as they were called, escaped to New York City.

Today Siculiana has re-invented itself as being THE place to get married, highlighted by a spectacular Spanish Castle from the 16th Century restored exactly for that reason.

Vita and I found the castle, toured it, and took a bunch of pictures of the nearby Chiesa Madre, Mother Church, and its beautiful statuary. We wandered about town for a while, and then continued on. I made a mental note to return here someday. There is a story about this town that needs to be told, I think, and I want to tell it.

From there, we headed to Sciacca.

Passing through Siculiana Marina, which was exquisite in its seafaring beauty and continuing to Secca, and then through Vedura… we arrived at perhaps the best fishing port in all of Sicily, the ancient town of Sciacca, our destination for this final day.

I had been here plenty of times because Paolo Licata, my friend from my All Things Sicilian days, had his production facility here, and I knew the area well.

Parking the car, we wandered the streets and Vita was amazed at the ceramic work on every corner.

This was an ancient town, once Phoenician, then Arabic, and the blending of the many varied and a diverse culture was everywhere.

We went to a great trattoria for lunch and had a terrific meal. This was one of those restaurants that has no menu; rather the owner sizes you up, and serves you food. Vita was impressed not only by the delicious seafood we ate, but also by the great wine decanter that we had on the table. She marveled at its beauty several times during the meal. It was ceramic, half liter in size, hand-painted.

We left the trattoria as two happy campers and continued to wander around. Vita found an old man playing the flute sitting on a park bench, and I must have shot a million photos of the two.

We headed to the port where Vita got out of the car and took many more pictures, and did I.

Some of my best shots were of her taking pictures. Even though it was scalding hot that day, there she was, in her bumble-bee sunglasses, jeans, and pink beret. The picture HAD to be taken.

On the way back to the car, I caught out of the corner of my eye a ceramic shop and ducked in. Ten minutes later I walked out with the wine pitcher that Vita had liked so much in the trattoria. She knew what I was up to, because her face was beaming as she opened the package. She was very happy, I can tell you that. She put the pitcher on the roof of the car, and photographed it from every angle. I bet she said thank you fifty times to me too. I was happy that she was happy.

Actually, I would have paid ten times more for it, truth be told.

Piling in the car, we started back. Even driving on the highway, it was going to be a long ride back.

Both of us had expended a tremendous amount of emotional energy on this road trip so far, and we were exhausted.

Little did I know that the ride home would be even more emotionally exhausting.

A Ride Home Like I Never Had Before.

I was the driver this trip, and Vita was the co-pilot. Although she repeatedly asked to drive, the macho in me constantly refused because, well, I am an idiot.

I knew she had a fierce independent streak and as we started back on the highway, with Valerie Giglio's music in the background, we started to talk.

One of things that I had asked her about was why she signed almost all her texts to me as "only Vita", as opposed to Vita, which was her name. The word "only" I told her in my best know it all lawyerly manner, has a negative connotation, and that I thought she was a special person, and that the word "only" was inappropriate. You are not an "only" I told her.

In her halting yet completely articulate English, she asked me if the word 'only" had a different meaning other that a negative one in this context. I mulled it over and told her that if she was a singular person and that if she meant to say that she was a self - imposed singular person, then yes, "only Vita" would be appropriate. It would mean that she chooses to be alone...she chooses to be "only Vita". Is this what she meant? Is that what she meant, that it just her and her alone?

That "only" Vita was created by design? That she wanted to be singular, stand alone?

She replied to me a single word: "Yes".

She then told me some personal things that I will not go into here. Suffice that my understanding of her became crystal clear. Her walls were up for justifiable reasons, and I realized that I was riding with a profoundly deep, spiritual, beautiful, inwardly emotional, and touching person. I realized as she talked that I too wanted to share something with her. Why, I do not know. Something in my soul told me "It's time".

So I did. I told her the story about Leonie. The complete, in depth story of a love lost about the love of my life, blow by blow, almost moment by moment, I told her the whole story. For the first time in a long time. To anyone. I told my story to only Vita.

It was like I had been transported back in time and that Leonie was sitting in the passenger seat as I was telling her what I had been feeling, thinking and grieving about all these years. In the pitch darkness while driving down a lonely highway in Sicily, with Valerie's music perfectly providing the background, a story hidden away for years came out.

I wept in front of a woman. I wept in front of a woman that I barely knew, something that I have fought a lifetime against. The tough guy. The street kid. The litigator. I am a tough guy litigator street kid from Lawrence Massachusetts and here I am, weeping. Weeping in front of a woman.

On that lonely road from Sciacca to Agrigento to Enna, and as we headed toward Catania, my soul was exposed.

I honestly do not know if I consciously realized that Vita was sitting next to me or what. All I know is that my soul felt emptied out and for the first time in a very long time, it did not feel heavy. I let go of something that night, not all of it, but something.

The next thing that I consciously realized was that Vita was tenderly stroking my arm.

For how long she did that, I did not know. However, when I realized what had happened, I was embarrassed and a little humiliated. "I am very sorry, Vita" I said. "I don't why I said that stuff".

She looked at me through the darkness of that night, and even in the pitch dark of the ride, I felt her eyes penetrating me. "You wanted to." She said. "You wanted to."

So that is the story of Alfred, *"only" Vita*, and our first road trip together across the southern Sicilian countryside over a two day period.

We saw more things that two could possibly see. We experienced things on many levels, we bonded into a friendship that I truly hope will last a very long time, and for me at least, the lock to my heart was now swinging open and the ghost that had been in there was stirring.

We stopped in Acitrezza just before midnight. We ate a bite, we had a lovely talk, we really enjoyed each other but in a friendly sort of way.

When I dropped her off at her hotel, I did not know what I felt. As a matter of fact, all the words I wanted to say were locked in my mouth. I need to watch myself and not stick my foot in my mouth.

In any event, she leaned over and kissed me on the cheek. A nice friendly kiss, one that was not a simple peck goodbye. Rather a friendly kiss from a person who really liked the other person.

"Thank you, Alfred" she said. "Maybe we can do this again soon."

What did she say? She wanted to do it again…with me? Another road trip? With me? Soon?

"I'll text you and see if I can get time off. Ciao," she said.

"Sure" I said. "That would be great." Then my heart smiled.

Chapter Eleven

The Time Between

For two days after the road trip, I laid low and processed things. That is my way of dealing with things of an emotional nature; retreat into myself and mull things over.

For two days I was awash in many different kinds of thoughts and I was working my way through each of them as I sat on my deck and gazing at the hazy Ionian Sea. Playing things over in my mind has always been helpful to me. The great view, the wonderful weather, and a cool off-shore breeze were healing indeed.

By the middle of the week, I sent Vita a text and invited her to dinner with me in Acitrezza, my glorious little fishing village that I call home. I was mulling over the possibility of taking a third road trip but thought maybe that I needed some emotional support on this one if I decided to take it.

I wanted to discuss it with her for her opinion.

She has mentioned to me that she loved eating pasta with nero di seppia, that wonderful sweet black tomato sauce made with the ink of the kuttle fish. In America, it is a delicacy. Around here, if you want to eat it, you come to Acitrezza because they have the best, and everyone knows it.

When I picked up Vita, she looked beautiful. She had on a simple black dress and looked completely different that she did on our road trip. No bumble bee glasses, no beret, no jeans. I pretended that we were going on a date. Why not? The Beauty and the Beast, I thought.

In Acitrezza before dinner, we walked along the *lungomare*, the equivalent to a boardwalk in America, and admired the rocks hurled by the Cyclops at Ulysses which were arranged very nicely offshore and had given birth to the Riviera dei Ciclopi tourist attraction.

Coupled with all the wooden lidos that had been constructed over the rocks creating temporary beaches that were safe and rock free (as well as sand free) folks flocked to sunbathe here and then to jump safely into the sea.

Homer's ancient work of the Odyssey had found a home in Acitrezza and Ulysses was practically its adopted son. Heck, the street I lived on was called Via Ulisse!

I took many photos of Vita by the rocks, and I think that she liked the attention that I was giving her. Put it this way, she didn't squawk about it as I was snapping away, that's for sure. I enjoyed the playfulness of the evening, two friends enjoying each other's company in a setting that belonged in a movie somewhere.

We ate dinner at the best fish restaurant in town that night and had a meal fit for royalty.

Appetizers of fresh shrimp, lightly floured and flash fried morsels of calamari, fresh anchovies in olive oil, garlic, parsley and lemon juice, frutti di mare…many other appetizer types of fish prepared in the tradition of the village inhabitants. For this night we shared a bottle of Prosecco bubbly wine with the main course which was the pasta with sepia.

The food was delicious, and we both decided that after driving all over the place in Sicily, the best food could be found a half mile away from my house. Go figure.

After dinner and over several drinks, and perhaps plied by the Prosecco bottle that was now empty as well as an after dinner aperitif, the conversation turned to that emotional ride home from Sciacca a couple days before. I was still embarrassed that I had spilled my emotions to her and I wanted to apologize again to her.

That is when I asked her to come with me to Amsterdam in September.

Dumbfounded, she asked why. I needed her emotional support and the story I told her that night was the reason why.

I intended to go to Holland one last time. Not to see Leonie, rather to say good bye to the place once and for all. I was ready to move on with my life, I had decided, and this last step of closure was necessary for me. I needed to close the door so another one, perhaps would open.

There was this little restaurant in Leiden, by the train station, that Leonie and I like to go for coffee and breakfast once a week. It was a handsome old Dutch restaurant, perhaps one hundred and fifty years old. The Dewe Egbert coffee served there was excellent, as were the omelets. Leonie loved that place and so did I.

In any case, I had decided that I would travel to Amsterdam, wander around the little village where I had my apartment one last time, go to this restaurant, have a coffee and bury the ghost of this part of my life once and for all.

I had found the cell number of Caroline, Leonie's sister and I planned to text her. I wanted her to let Leonie know that on a certain date and a certain time in September, I would be at this restaurant drinking coffee, and that maybe Leonie could come and join me.

I knew that Caroline would never tell Leonie that I would be there. The family was now way too protective, but I wanted her to know in any case. I would tell Caroline that I would wait at the restaurant from 11am to 1PM, and then leave. For two hours I would sit and remember.

In my mind, when I got up to leave, I would close the book on this chapter of my life forever, and move on.

I told Vita that something happened to me on that road trip that now made me want to do this. It was time and I was ready. I wanted Vita there with me for emotional support, I guess. This would be emotional enough for me, and since she was the only one I had shared my emotions with, I wanted her with me.

Funny, I wasn't emotional when I was talking to Vita about this. Rather, my vision was out of focus, I was imagining myself sitting at that restaurant in Leiden when I was talking to Vita. I was far away as I spoke. I was in Amsterdam in my head while I was talking to Vita in Acitrezza, if you can understand what I mean.

When I finished my little story, my vision returned to where I was sitting in the restaurant. It came back into focus. Vita was the one with tears rolling down her cheeks now. She told me that this was a beautiful thing I wanted to do, but it was something I had to do by myself. I had to do this alone, she said. She was happy that I wanted her there, I think, but no, you must do this by yourself.

That night felt like a date to me, to tell you the truth. I respected her space, and I knew that nothing had changed as far as she was concerned as far as her feelings were concerned, but really…we were way past the stage of a friendship in my mind. I understood the boundaries that she established, but what was transpiring between us was something that now had no valid definition in terms of a verbal description of our agreed word…"friendship". I was searching for a more concise word than friendship, but I could not and I still can't put my finger on it.

It was a great night, with a great person, in a great environment and we both deepened this friendship. Later we dropped by Roberto's place in Naxos for a nightcap and then I reluctantly left. What is with this? Every time I am with this woman, it seems, I didn't want the night to end. Very strange things were going on in my brain, very strange things indeed.

A couple days later we went to the circus along with two of Vita's friends. We went to Acireale to the sports stadium and saw the Cirque Du Soleil perform Saltimbanco.

Have you ever seen the Cirque Du Soleil? If you haven't, it needs to be put on your list of things to do. I bought the CD, and two tunes, Kumbalawe and Horere Ukunde transport me to a faraway place every time I hear them.

However, I was very distracted that night. Very distracted.

Well, the next morning, Vita and I were leaving for our second two-day road trip, and I was excited as hell.

A trip for the ages was about to happen to me, and I knew it this time, and I was excited.

Well, turn the page and I will tell you about it. Why not? I have told you far too much already, and at this point you are probably curious, no?

Chapter Twelve

On the Road Again With Vita and How I Became "Only "Alfred

To be honest with you, I was both anxious and frightened for the road trip to begin. I was looking forward to starting it, but was kind of dreading its ending. I was anxious is a good way. I knew the next two days with Vita and the Sicilian landscape would be wondrous and unforgettable, and Vita was leaving for Rhodes, Greece's biggest island, on Friday. She wasn't sure if she would ever return to Sicily.

I did not know if I would ever see her again after this week.

She had told me that she was 99% sure that she would go to Spain after the summer, so I didn't know if the two days that I would spend with her would be the last two days that I would ever spend with her or what. The odds were long against ever seeing her again, and I was grieving over that.

I was torn. A sweet beginning, but a bitter end was in sight no matter what I could do or say or hope for. I knew this weeks ago. However, that was weeks ago, and now, and within a matter of days, she would disappear into the wind.

I had decided to pretend that these two days were the last two days of my life, and that I would live them second by second, minute by minute. Why not? Isn't that the Sicilian way? Live each day as if it's your last, right?

Vita was an athlete. She was an accomplished swimmer who swam competitively for her country, Lithuania, for years. She was also a ranked skier for her country, a bungee jumper, and a scuba diver. Greece had some of the world's best scuba diving. Its rich history and sudden sea storms had established Rhodes as perhaps the finest scuba diving area in Europe. When she didn't work, she and her friends engaged in all things athletic. She worked hard, but she played hard too. Rhodes was calling her again.

I too was an athlete, but that was years ago. I played college football, and I threw the shot put, discus, played basketball in high school and had coached athletes for many years at many levels. I understood her. I know what it is like to want adventure.

Thus, every minute with her on this trip would be a treasured time. I was well aware about seeing someone again and then not seeing the same person. It had happened to me once with Leonie, and this time I knew going in what the story was.

To me, this is a BIG difference. With Vita, I knew this may be it. With Leonie, her aneurysms were unexpected. I saw nothing coming. Nothing.

The plan was to take the autostrada around Messina directly to Milazzo, then find a back parallel road and travel to Tindari to see the Shrine of the Black Madonna. Afterward, we would then continue west and try to get as far as could that first day.

Santo Stefano di Camastra seemed like a logical objective for our first day's destination, and then the following day it would be a straight shot to Castellammare del Golfo and San Vito lo Capo on the west coast. The plan was to eat couscous at San Vito lo Capo, and then head home.

It was an ambitious itinerary, but we figured we would give it our best shot.

When I picked up Vita from her hotel, she looked completely different than she had on the last trip.

Her jeans and beret had been replaced with a beautiful light summer Lithuanian dress that was very colorful, a scarf round her neck, and one of those Arabic head things that the women in Muslim countries wear. She looked sultry, alluring, beautiful and also very European. I thought it was a very cool look and I complimented her on it.

This time, she knew exactly what she wanted to hear on the iPod, and in no time flat, she was the DJ matching perfectly the music with the scenery. We both were comfortable with each other now, and knew what to expect in terms of emotional attachment and energy expenditure. The trip would be exhilarating, exhausting, fun, and the unknown was lurking somewhere too.

Many wonderful things would happen on that first magical first day.

When we got to Milazzo, we jumped off the highway and found a lovely country road (Route 113) that quickly took us to the sea. This time, the sea was on our right, and the terrain was hilly. It seemed we were going up one steep hill and down another into one magnificent valley after another yet to climb up another steep hill that was followed by yet another magnificent valley.

We hardly spoke. There was no need to. The music that we were playing and the visual beauty we were experiencing were enough. They spoke volumes to each of us, and we were listening and enjoying the moment. The Magic Carpet was operating at peak efficiently again and two kindred souls were once again sharing a great experience.

We traveled through the beautiful villages of Caldera, Castroreale Terme, Tonnarella, Falcone and Oliveri all the while stopping to look at things, buy fresh cherries, water and the like. Then we started the very steep ascent towards Tindari…sitting high atop a mountain overlooking the sea.

This section of Sicily is lush, the bounty of the back side of Etna evident everywhere.

Every few kilometers or so, roadside fruit sellers were selling what they had picked that day.

Cherries were just being harvested and were selling for 2.50 euro a kilo. They were delicious. Peaches, plums, nespole, you name it, was on the carts and for sale that day.

The day was rapidly heating up, and even as we climbed toward Tindari, we knew that we were in for a very hot day. By 11am in the morning, the temperature was close to 90 degrees.

Arriving at Tindari, we parked the car and took the bus up the road to the Basilica of the Black Madonna. The village was completely dependent on the tourist dollar, so souvenir stands were everywhere and people were selling replicas of the Black Madonna, nuts, necklaces, you name it, all over the place.

In the states, some of this stuff would sell for big money, but here, during "La Crisi" (the Crisis), which was the term used by Sicilians for the recession/depression/financial disaster that was gripping Europe and the world, everything could be had for cut rate prices.

Vita was hungry so we decided to first find a place and grab a bite to eat at a trattoria near the Basilica. Vita had arancini and I had my usual salad. We shared a carafe of white wine.

Earlier, I had purchased for Vita a necklace made from hazelnuts from a vendor while walking to the trattoria …hazelnuts grew abundantly in this area…and while we were waiting for our food, Vita began to eat the necklace…just like a child would do!

By the time lunch was served, the necklace was completely gone and we both got a good laugh about this. On the way down to the car later in the day, I got her another. I took a bunch of great pictures of her munching on that necklace too!

The Basilica of the Black Madonna is a spiritual place and a holy place. We toured the sacristy in the back, and I took some great photos. Outside the Basilica, on a beautiful ledge overlooking the valley, I took some wonderful shots both of the landscape and of Vita.

Did I tell you that by this time, my ratio of pictures had gone from 90% pictures of the Sicilian countryside and 10% pictures of Vita to an even 50-50%? Yup. In the history of my life, I had never photographed one person so many times. But honesty, I had a great time, and they all were great shots.

I did not know that shortly one of my life's defining moments was about to happen to me. At this point in our journey, we were happy and content. Two souls enjoying a great journey and each other's company, in a friendly sort of way.

I have been studying the map of the route we took that day -Route 113 - trying to pinpoint the exact spot where the ghost that had haunting me for all these years finally left me. You see, somewhere along Route 113 on a hot Sicilian day, on the road from Tindari to Santo Stefano, my life changed.

Not only would it change, but the decision that I had made about going to Amsterdam would fade into oblivion. It would no longer be necessary.

On this day, somewhere between Tindari and I think Sant' Agata di Militello, on the road that day to Santo Stefano di Camastra... maybe it was Capo d'Orlando...one of life's defining moments took place for me.

A moment so tender, so unforgettable, that when I later recounted it to my friend Valerie Giglio the singer, she was reduced to tears, and she told to me that my story gave her a renewed sense of love and motivation for her singing and song writing. She is even writing a song about what transpired.

I will now try to paint a picture for you of that moment, but I know that I will fail miserably.

However, I owe it to myself, I owe it to Vita, and I owe it to the memory of a love lost to attempt to do so.

Forgive me as I now attempt to re-create a wonderful moment in time.

As we left Tindari, the heat was really at its highest of the day. It was probably 95 degrees outside.

We were hugging the sea by following Route 113, a beautiful little two lane roadway that previously served as a major transit artery between Messina and Palermo long before the autostrada was built. For us on this day it was perfect. No traffic, excellent visibility, a slight sea breeze to cool us down a little, and great music playing on the iPod tying everything together.

Vita and I were in our non-verbal communication stage. We were so busy enjoying the cascading scenery that differed around each bend and twist of roadway that there was nothing really to say.

We were on the exact same wave length that moment. Which really wasn't a moment at all. Rather, more like an hour. But time had long stopped still for me.

Our magic carpet ride was entering its finest phase, a magical ride if there was ever to be one, enhanced by the beauty of each succeeding village and wayside on that stretch of road that day.

At some point, the elevation of the road got higher. Over perhaps a ten- mile stretch, we were up pretty high along the roadway, with the sea still being on our right, and distance below enormous.

The panoramic vistas and sights were getting to be metaphysical. Surreal, actually. Vita was doing an excellent job of selecting the music by now, as she knew what songs she liked, and where they were located on the iPod. The music that she selected could not have been better even if Mozart had been riding in the back seat.

As we turned a long and winding corner, the view broke into a spectacular sight. On one side was the vista of the sea below and on the other side was a view of the Sicilian countryside below.

We were high in the heavens, it seemed, looking down on earth.

Vita had just put on Valerie's cover of the famous love song "Caruso"...that haunting and soulful song so brilliantly performed by Valerie it seemed just for us on that day, and out of nowhere a spot appeared where I could pull the car off the road. Here, we could appreciate the special setting that was unfolding before our eyes.

Simultaneously, we each opened our door and got out...I walked in one direction to admire what I was seeing, and Vita in another. The iPod was still playing Caruso and the music...the haunting music... was playing in the background.

My back was turned to Vita, and hers to mine. Then we turned almost at the same time and looked at each other. How this happened I do not know. It wasn't planned, that is for sure.

In the searing heat of that day, along the vista view area where I had pulled the car over, in broad daylight, and with passing cars looking at us with quizzical looks on their faces, we danced ...to the sweetest of melodies playing only to our ears.

I clutched her tightly. I clutched tightly a woman who had admonished me not to do that because we were friends and that she didn't feel anything for me "in that way" and I think she did the same.

For a nanosecond, the rule was broken.

I cannot say for sure how long that moment lasted. One minute? Two minutes? I know that I was not dancing alone, I can tell you that with certainty. We were both holding on to something, something important and something very special. Was I dancing with Vita? Was I saying good-bye to Leonie? Exactly what the hell was happening to me?

Well, reality got a hold of me after several moments, and I opened my eyes and awkwardly released Vita and quickly got back in the car.

I was struggling with my emotions again. What in God's name had just happened? Why did it happen? The computer in my head did not understand.

Vita returned to the car and got in.

I apologized to Vita, and told her that I did not know what came over me. She looked at me and told me that there was nothing to apologize about. It wasn't what she said; it was what she didn't say.

I do not know what she was feeling or what she was thinking, but I do know that she leaned over and re-played that song again as we drove off.

In silence and lost in our thoughts, we did not speak for a very long time. I was a million miles away, and so was she. Two hours later we pulled into a hotel in Santo Stefano for the night. We swam, we dined at a good restaurant, we had a long emotional talk, and then we slept.

I processed those two minutes that we danced all night long. I think she did, too. To me, the instant when I touched her and we danced, was the moment that my life, my emotional life, started again.

The chains to my heart broke, I threw them away, and I was freed from my prison, at last.

This remarkable women had helped me to this. My "friend," my "only" Vita. Which, by the way, is now a ridiculous way to describe her. So that was the story of the first day of our last two day road trip together. Enough emotion to last three lifetimes.

However, the story isn't over yet.

Now, I must rest a bit and contemplate again what happened to us before I can continue. I bet you thought this was going to be a regular tour book, didn't you? Well, as it turns out, it is not.

Day Two

The plan for day two was straightforward or so I thought. Then again, nothing that happened with Vita was straightforward. By this time any expectation that I had going in had gone out the window and I was pretty much in it for the ride.

In any case, we decided to high-tail directly to Castellammare del Golfo and completely by pass Palermo. We would accomplish this phase of the trip, and save time, by jumping on the autostrada and getting off by Castellammare del Golfo, and then taking the back roads into San Vito lo Capo, our destination. All of this in order to eat couscous for lunch, which Vita loved.

Before we left we had a very special time walking the back streets together of Santo Stefano and poking around the great ceramic shops of this beautiful little town.

Vita was dressed in her bumble-bee outfit again with her huge sun glasses, jeans, a light top and her ever present beret. I remember this because she was in a very playful mood all morning long, and one time as she was drinking from an ancient water fountain, turned and splashed me. I caught the episode on my camera too, and I was happy for the special moment.

Soon we left town, but this time Vita insisted that today she would drive. She said I drove in the middle of the road all the time (which I do) and she would show me how to drive. I would be in charge of the music today she said. I explained to her what a big responsibility driving my beat up Punto was, and how powerful the egg-beater really was.

As a matter of fact, as she started the car for the first time, I played the part of an Alitalia pilot talking to the passengers just before take-off. "Good morning ladies and gentlemen, on behalf of Alitalia airlines and your Captain Vita, thank you for flying with us - sit back and relax…."

I made up a whole skit that had her laughing.

Seriously, she was a skillful driver. Better than I. (sigh)

Little did I know that this day would be divided into two separate parts: the first part consisting of a joyful time together as we proceeded down the highway to our destination and…well…I will wait a bit and tell you about the second part of the day.

Have you ever seen the vista view from Castellammare del Golfo? Google it. It is the finest view of the coastline in all of Sicily, and perhaps in all of Europe. This is a special place that needs to be seen by every visitor to Sicily. We both had been here a bunch of times, but no trip out this far west is complete without a visit to the viewpoint.

At the top of a long hill climb is the area that you can stop the car and take pictures - you can even get a bite to eat from the roadside vendors there. While this picturesque and magnificent view was indeed special for me this day, it was special for me for another reason. Today I had the foresight to ask a passer-by to take a photo of both Vita and I together. He took two. I was happy to look at them later see them because we were both happy that day, and the pictures showed that very clearly.

I was also happy for another reason. These two pictures are only the third or fourth pictures that capture us in the same image. They are kind of special to me, truth be told, and made the trip up to this vista worth it.

The day was brilliant, sunny and hot. We were ready to embark on our final leg of the journey to San Vito lo Capo for lunch, maybe lay on the beach and swim for awhile and then begin the long journey home.

Today was turning out to be yet another magical day, the Magic Carpet humming along, and two spirits enjoying the surrounding countryside and companionship in a friendly sort of way. From Castellammare, we wound through all the back roads toward San Vito lo Capo. The terrain was becoming increasingly barren, rocky, and reminded me of a moonscape.

We travelled through Puntazza, then veered slightly west toward Luppino, Castelluzzo, Timpone, Purgatorio, San Giuseppe and finally we hit San Vito lo Capo. All small barren towns on rocky terrain.

Of all the areas we had seen, this ride was the most arid, barren and lonely of all. San Vito lo Capo was the oasis, and we were going to enjoy ourselves for a few hours. San Vito lo Capo is perhaps one of the nicest beach resorts on the western side of the island. Its sole drawback is that its white sand beaches are well known and packed with tourists, most of them are from the European continent. Nonetheless I wanted to show Vita this place because it also is home to some of Sicily's best couscous restaurants. Vita told me that when she was in Egypt she ate couscous often and really wanted to try the Sicilian version.

I stopped a local police officer and asked her where we could find a good couscous restaurant, and she directed us to a restaurant named Syrah. After walking for perhaps ten minutes down the main thoroughfare, we found this great little restaurant and proceeded to have the best couscous meal, ever.

We both had the fish couscous and the "brodo" (fish broth) was spectacular, as were the huge and tender chunks of fish on top of the couscous. If this place were in Boston or New York City, the lines would be blocks long. Here, we were practically the only ones in the restaurant.

Some of the happiest pictures of Vita that I snapped were of here rolling up the couscous into little balls with her fingers, like they do in North Africa, and eating it that way. I used a fork, but she ate it the Arabic way.

I later told someone that the food was so delicious that this restaurant, by itself, was worth the drive clear across the island for... it was that good.

We had packed our bathing suits, and after lunch changed into our swim wear and hit the beach for an hour to swim the beautiful waters of this area. Just to say that we did. Vita thought the beach was too packed to really enjoy herself. She enjoyed the solitude of the other places we went, but was a good sport about the beach.

After cleaning up and having a gelato at a gelateria, it was time to head back.

The Ride Back Home

I began to detect a subtle change in Vita the minute she started up the car to head back.

To me, she was beginning to withdraw into a shell a little. I thought it was my imagination at first. Maybe I had said something to piss her off. Maybe she was tired. Whatever it was, I could feel her walls going up and she was beginning to withdraw back into herself ever so slowly.

She was leaving for Greece in three days, and I did not know if I ever would see her again.

This is what was beginning to weigh me down a bit.

I never wanted the road trip to end. Vita had inadvertently caused me to have a paradigm shift within myself, she had been the sole reason that I let go of a precious yet deadly memory and had freed my soul. She had done this. No, we had done this. At "arms length" and in a "friendly way," as she was constantly telling me.

All I knew was that in three days I wasn't going to see her anymore. The reality was beginning to hit home once we started back to

Naxos. She asked me to put the music on. By this time, the sun was setting, and it was that time of day I call *sfumato* or smokey, when the sun is beginning to go to sleep and darkness begins to envelop space.

I mindlessly hit the playlist, not really caring what tune came on at this point because I too wanted to get lost into myself. I think I was starting to grieve Vita, to be honest. Valerie's CD came on.

In silence her music cut my soul in half, and then cut it in half again. I sighed deeply and in the *sfumato* darkness glanced at Vita.

Tears were rolling down her cheeks.

In silence on the highway heading back to Naxos on that warm summer night, listening to the very same music that compelled me to tears a scant week earlier, tears were now flowing from Vita.

I touched her cheeks and wiped away a tear. She was stoic. She said not one word. Valerie's song finished. Vita asked that it I re-play it. I did.

In silence her tears still came like daggers sticking repeatedly in my heart. Was she thinking about a love lost? Was she thinking about leaving Sicily? Was she feeling sorry that her feelings for me were not "feelings"? What? What was happening to this magnificent creature on that dark and lonely road back to Naxos that night?

Baltic people are intensely private, and after the third time asking her, I stopped.

I think either I touched her soul, or my story did. This is what I want to believe. She is my forever friend. Yes, I probably do love her, in violation of the Jennifer Rule, and probably the laws of man. Tough luck. I am who I am and I feel what I feel.

She does not have to love me back. I love Vita because she was the path that was sent to free my soul. If she had indeed loved me, that would have been extra, I think. It made no difference. None at all. I loved Vita at arm's length and in a friendly manner per her request. This gentle, spiritual soul had reached inside me and touched my soul and released the spirit.

How could I not love this person?

When I dropped her off at the hotel, we practically said nothing to each other. What could I possibly say to her and vice versa? We held each other tightly in a borderline friendly way. A lot of emotions were exchanged between us that remained silent, unsaid.

By then Vita had transformed herself back into *"only" Vita* again.

By then, her emotional defenses were up and operational. I completely understood her now. I accepted this.

I saw Vita one more time at Roberto's the night before she left.

She was with friends. I didn't want to disturb her time with them, so I just very briefly interrupted her at the table she was sitting at and said goodbye and wished her well.

Then I left. I was free, at last, from the spirit of Leonie.

What was really left, though, was "*only*" *Alfred*. Vita helped me see this. I am now *"only Alfred"*, and we shall see what we shall see, won't we?

And that is the story of "*only Vita*", the most remarkable person ever to cross my path in life.

Then again.....the story, as I would find out later...was not yet over. For now, however, sadly it was.

Alfred and Roberto at Café Sikelia.

Farmland beauty.

Motta Camastra

Castiglione di Sicilia

Above: Leonforte
Below: Buccheri

Above: A common sight on roads aroound Mt. Etna.
Below: Heaven on earth... Buccheri

Above: Vita

Below: Vita in Tindari

Marzamemi:

The two travelers... in Portopalo

Bay of Portopalo di Capo Passero.

Portopalo di Capo Passero.

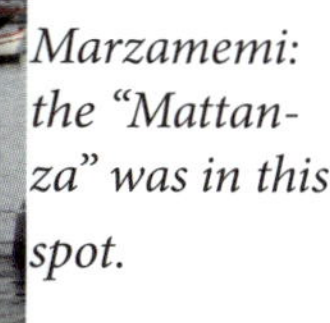

Marzamemi: the "Mattanza" was in this spot.

Example of Noto's Baroque architecture.

The Castello di Calatabiano

Marzamemi where the tuna from the "mattanza" were processed.

Above: Motta Camastra.
Below: Beautiful towns on the backside of Mt. Etna.

Above: View from Don Santo's Trattoria.
Below: View from the Castello di Calatabiano.

Parco botanico e geologico delle Gole dell'Alcantara.

Another view from the Castello di Calatabiano.

Chapter Thirteen

Prequel: The First Ping of the Heart
Gabriella: Pointing Me in the Right Direction

Introduction:

For the last several chapters I introduced you to "*only Vita*" and re-counted for you the journeys that we took together and how those journeys essentially fixed my heart and opened my soul. Vita helped me re-enter the human race, but a person before Vita started the process, and I must now write about her in the Sicilian context.

I am convinced that Sicily and the environment created by her magnificence was the primary reason for my emotional re-birth, but I believe also that the confluence of special people, such as Vita and Gabri (who you will soon meet) entered that paradigm at that exact moment enabled it to happen. Thus Sicily is, was and will forever be, the setting, and the people there that I met were and will forever be the agents of change for me.

Recall that with Vita the backdrop was Piazza Armerina, Gela, Agrigento, Naxos, San Vito lo Capo, Sciacca, Santo Stefano to name just a few.

With Gabriella, my relationship with her occurred primarily with the confines of Aci Catena, Acitrezza, Catania, Floridia (not the American state…rather the little town just outside Siracusa) and finally the United States itself.

In my chapters about only Vita, she was the end game, the final entry into my life that completed my healing. My relationship with Vita was a sensory one; the sights and textures of the Sicilian countryside having an intense affect on the relationship.

With Gabriella, the relationship was an intellectual one. One based on verbal communication and physical touch and fury and passion and sadness and many other emotions that were lost along the way of life by me.

Gabriella got the ball rolling for me in my re-birth, and I will always love her, respect her, and honor her spirit and intellect. Truth be told, she is my hero now. A remarkable gift from God sent to me in order to show me the way out of my personal despair.

Here is Gabriella…or Gabri as I call her… and I will tell you the story of a courageous woman who first pinged my heart the year before I met Vita. The woman who first awakened long dormant feelings in me…however briefly…and set forth in motion the recovery that was needed to salvage my emotional well being.

Gabriella is a profound intellect, and as it turns out, a gift from the angels that I regard today in the highest of esteem.

This is Gabri's story and I am happy that I am going to tell you about her.

First though, you need to know the background leading up to our meeting and subsequent relationship.

Did I tell you that when I first met her she was homeless? Well, you are going to love this tale.

Background: January 2011

2010 was a disaster for me. Actually, so was 2009 and 2008.

I was on a three year losing streak that was in the process of wiping out a lifetime of savings, ruining my health, was one of the reasons that my wife had thrown up her hands up and finally walked out on me, and to top it off, business failings had caused me lose a lifetime of friends.

The economic downturn that gripped the world was in the process of killing my pride and joy in life. My business, All Things Sicilian, which I had started along with a small group of friends/investors was tanking and there was nothing I could do about it.

We had started All Things Sicilian in 2000 and I was the point man on the project. It was my idea originally and my law partner Massimo and I had made all the contacts in Sicily for the many wonderful products that we were to import into America. My friends who were of Sicilian background, many of them successful professionals in their own right, were eager to invest in the idea.

No one had the vision that I had about this idea, and everyone in those days was flush with money. The economic downturn hadn't yet reared its ugly head and people were investing money into these types of investments. And, my friends had money to invest.

For the first several years after opening the business, we grew by leaps and bounds.

Thousands of people were enamored in "All Things Sicilian" and loved what we were doing. Within three years, we had opened three retail stores, a huge internet business and a wholesale operation that supplied our products to stores everywhere.

The prospects looked great, the signs were encouraging, and everyone was happy.

Then, disaster stuck.

We had committed the cardinal sin of a new business: over confidence and under capitalization. Throw in a dash of lack of experience plus bad decisions all around and you guessed it…in short order we were popular with the customers but cash poor. We had over extended ourselves with no cushion to fall back on.

Encouraged by our initial success, we expanded too quickly.

In retrospect, we should not have done this. We should have stockpiled our profits, and grown naturally. However, in those years, the American economy was humming along, the dollar was strong against the euro and not only was America strong, but so was the European economy.

In Sicily, the Italian government was lending hundreds of millions of euro to businesses in the hopes of establishing markets in America, Asia, and the world.

We felt that we were doing our part in America and people's imaginations were being captivated. We felt that we had lightening in a bottle.

Then September 11, 2001 occurred. In rapid succession, the Afghanistan invasion took place, the Iraq war began, and America pre-September 11, 2001 was gone and a new reality created.

Vitriol in politics was the operative word in America as things deteriorated. The *coup de grace,* so to speak, was the Wall Street debacle in 2007 which caused the housing crisis and the dollar to lose much of its value. Unemployment spiked and the US and the world was now on the brink of the greatest calamity since the Great Depression.

When things started to go bad, and not understanding the complexity of what was going on (really…at that time, were there many people who DID realize the complexity and urgency of danger that was about to befall us?), I foolishly plodded on. I thought that with hard work, the problems that were happening with All Things Sicilian would solve themselves.

Wasn't that the American way, I thought? Would not hard work solve all problems?

Well, as it turned out, no it wasn't.

In rapid succession, business revenues nose dived as customers stopped purchasing expensive imported products. Banks would not loan us any more money (as it turns out, they had lost it all, but in those days who knew?), and my small group of investors were also depleted of cash.

With no safety net, the handwriting was on the wall for All Things Sicilian, unfortunately. The till was empty.

For four years, I refused to believe this. For four years, I blocked out everything in my life and worked countless hours in a futile attempt to stop the out of control business that was now careening in an unrelenting downward spiral.

Many things happen when things go bad for an extended period, it seemed, and they were all happening to me.

Lifelong friendships evaporated in front of my eyes as investment monies were lost (I later concluded that many of these relationships were businesses relationships and not friendships because a handful of people who originally started with me in All Things Sicilian still are my dear friends...but several others, unfortunately became bitter by the experience).

Thus, my savings were lost and finally my marriage fell apart. I want to quantify something about this marriage; while my financial ruination was the coup de grace to the marriage, my emotional detachment, I later learned was the real reason. I was incapable of loving at this time in my life, but back then I was oblivious to that.

Two positives remained for me at this time that preserved my sanity and ultimately opened the path to salvation for me.

The first was teaching at my beloved law schools. Teaching was always my saving grace. It provided funds for me to live and was my island of tranquility. And, I was very good at it. My reputation as a bar exam expert was nationwide. The second good thing that happened was that I had found Sicily.

By 2000 I was regularly traveling there for business purposes, and over time developed a vast network of friends and contacts. Most importantly, as things got worse in America, Sicily became my mistress who sheltered me, nurtured me, protected me, and who ultimately healed me.

Of course, by early 2011 none of these things had yet been processed by me. All I knew was that I had lost a small fortune, my friends hated me, my wife had walked out on me, and I felt terrible.

I decided to go to Sicily for Capod'anno (New Year's Eve) and try to ring in 2011 on as positive a note as possible. Mainly I went there to try to get a respite from all these problems.

In 2002 I had experienced the devastation of my life as my then wife Leonie had suffered her aneurysms and I was still working my way through those emotional issues…and then this devastation occurred several years later.

Unknown to me at that time, the stress of life had taken its toll… unknown to me back then …and would not be known by me for several more years…was that I had a ticking time bomb in my heart.

A serious heart condition had developed because of all this stress, and I was oblivious to it.

With this background, now you can meet Gabriella.

Gabriella

The first thing I should tell you about Gabriella is that when I first met her, she was homeless and had been taken in by a friend.

She had no steady job except the occasional English lessons that she gave Sicilian kids, or the money that she earned cleaning the apartments of American servicemen from Sigonella with whom she was friendly. Being 43 years old, it would prove nearly impossible for her to find employment in Sicily. Last year, I wrote a story about a woman trying to find work in *"Gaetano's Trunk"*. I can tell you today, that woman was Gabriella.

Gabriella had experienced a series of personal problems throughout her life and had recently emerged from the depths of despair after being lost there for two decades. She has emerged from her trials of life a stronger and more enlightened soul, and it was at this period of her life that we met in January of 2011.

Her problems behind her, she was trying now to find her worth in life. She was (and still is) a beautiful person. Maybe not beautiful in the truest of physical senses (does that really matter?), but her beauty was compelling to me as time passed and I got to know her. At a certain point in time, I saw only her soul and talked to that.

She was a simple Sicilian woman, as she would tell me, content to do meager jobs during the week. Content with just enough to give her money to feed herself and keep gas in her scooter. This was her reality. Material possessions meant little to her and she was content wearing the hand me down clothing of friends.

Friday nights were hugely important to her. That is when she and her friend would get all dolled up, and go and party at Go-Go's, a bar in Acitrezza.

They would party hard. Very hard. Too hard. Hard enough to cause me worry as a matter of fact.

She would shed that cloistered existence that she maintained during the week and for a few hours every week she would become extroverted. I still do not know what it was, the safety of Go-Go or the friends she had, or maybe the alcohol she drank. Perhaps it was the confluence of the three. But every Friday night, another persona was created.

She was 43 and single when I met her. She was a late-in-life medical student now attending part time at the University Of Catania Medical School. She had completed her academic course load but was struggling now to pass her oral exams. She was a brilliant intellect but clammed up when the professor's asked her oral test questions that were necessary to pass the course.

I once saw her recite thirty consecutive pages from her text book on blood disorders yet she failed the exam the next day because her mouth would not open to let out even a single word.

Was she beautiful in the context of a knock-out Sicilian beauty? No. However, she was the most beautiful woman I spiritually that I had met in a long time.

Her beauty came from within; her soul which had suffered a series of devastating events years before which had destroyed her mentally and physically, was still intact and emerging stronger after a twenty year struggle with demons in her head.

She emerged victorious in a struggle that had conquered many. She was perfect.

This middle-aged, homeless, Sicilian woman, as it turns out, would be a very compelling figure in my life, and would be the primary person responsible for my decision to try to do something to help the Sicilian people. Gabriella, you see, was my Ground Zero for the creation of the Sicilian Project which today is in the process of teaching English to many students in Sicily. She was my motivation to get this project off the ground. She showed me that Sicily needed this.

Gabriella's voice (in my mind, I go back and forth between "Gabriella" as her name …which it is…and "Gabri" which is the name I later called her affectionately), still reverberates in my mind. I hear it to this day in my mind's eye.

Yes, we had a brief relationship of the heart that lasted several months. Yes, it was intense. But yes, that part of our relationship ended and mutated into something else.

After our relationship was over, I reverted back to calling her "Gabriella"…although in my heart, for some reason, she is still "Gabri". Try figuring that one out…I cannot.

I first met her as she was sitting on the deck of my next-door neighbor smoking a cigarette. I conduct a lot of my business as I sit on my deck in my house in Aci Catena, and on this day, she was sitting on the adjacent deck shrouded in a blanket from head to toe. I said good morning to her as I paced back and forth on my deck between one of my phone calls, but she said nothing.

The next day, the same thing occurred. We gazed at each other but said nothing.

By the third day, when our eyes again locked briefly, we spoke for the first time.

I greeted her and she responded. She was still shrouded beneath that blanket. Her voice sounded like that of an angel, sweet, soft, soothing, comforting, spiritual, calm…an exact reflection of her personality

I would soon learn.

We exchanged a few words. I asked her name, we talked small talk for a while. She told me she was born in the states but moved to a small town on the outskirts of Siracusa named Florida. She had moved to Sicily when she was a child of twelve. Her English was nearly perfect, no accent that I could notice.

She told me that she was a medical student but had taught English off and on for twenty years privately and at language schools in Catania and the surrounding areas.

An hour or two flew by as we had that first conversation.

I liked her. She was a breath of fresh air and I wanted to talk to her longer.

Unfortunately, I had a business appointment and had to leave. However, I invited her over to my place later on that evening for a drink with friends that I had coming over and she told me that she would think about it. She had plans that night, but would let me know. I gave her my telephone number and we said our good-bye's.

I remember being kind of smitten by this homeless waif for some reason. I could not put my finger on it.

I do not know why. Something pinged in my heart. It was a feeling that I had not had in a decade. Like one of those sounds that we see in a war movie about submarines, the sound was faint but growing stronger.

Gabri came over my house that night, and yes, we kissed for the first time. Like a teenager, I kissed her, and she embraced me too. It was a silly, awkward yet tender moment.

Later that night, after Gabri had left my house, I penned the following essay to myself: I called it *The Sicilian Woman.*

Before we go on, you should read it.

It will help you understand. It tells briefly what happened that night when she came to the house.

Message to myself: The Sicilian Woman. Written after first meeting Gabriella. What does this mean, Alfred?

Something about her attracted me from the first time I gazed at her. Something compelling. In a split second, this woman entered the deepest recesses of my soul. And I didn't even know her name. I said "buongiorno" to her. She said nothing.

She was on the deck of the next-door neighbor and I was on mine, ten feet away. I had been talking to a client on the cell phone and turned to see her. Nothing. She said nothing.

She was covered with a blanket that morning and I could see nothing but the eyes. The blanket was draped around her as she struggled to keep warm as she smoked that cigarette.

The eyes. They entered my soul in a nano second. And I didn't know her name. Did she have a voice I wondered?

Several days passed and again on the deck of the neighbor sat this woman; still shrouded in mystery. Again I greeted her.

"I am sorry that I said nothing to you the last time" she said. "I didn't know if you were talking to me or the person on the phone."

The eyes. Again they drilled me. This time she revealed the face. She had dropped her shroud to talk to me.

It was a familiar face. A face that I had seen in a previous life. A remarkable face not so much for its beauty, but for what it was hiding.

We talked. I was attracted to her. Her spirit compelled me. I was attracted first to her soul. She is smart…borderline brilliant. I am excited to feel this way. It has been a long time. Too long.

Several times while talking to her, I fell over my words. Only once this had happened…when I met Leonie that first night in Naxos. I never fall over my words. I control words. I create them. At this moment, I fell over my words. I asked her age. She told me. She asked my age and I told her. I briefly I thought about telling her a younger one. I didn't. I told the truth.

Somehow, I connected with her. I could feel it with every molecule in my body. She had a story to tell and she chose me. An hour passed. We talked. I learned about her. She is a waif. She needs help but strangely is happy in her skin. It makes no difference the physical things in life. None whatsoever. How strange, I thought.

I had to leave. Damn business appointment.

I took a leap of faith and invited her over to my house for a glass of wine later tonight evening. I was having friends over. I wanted her there.

"I have plans tonight" she said. "But let me think about it."

Later that afternoon, my cell phone rang. "It's Gabriella" she said. Gabriella.

Her name. That is the name of an angel. She will become my angel, I thought.

"I can come over about 8 tonight but can stay only for a little while" she said.

I was happy. Very happy. An angel would come to visit.

That afternoon, I became a teenager again. I was excited. A certain anticipation had taken over my mind, my soul. I hadn't felt like this in a long time…and I could not understand why I was feeling like this. Usually, this type of a person I would not give two seconds of my life to, but I found myself craving to know everything about this one.

"I know nothing about this woman," I thought. "But I know everything" That night we kissed for the first time. It was a deep spiritual kiss that awakened long dormant feelings in my soul.

Sicily had sent me an angel in my darkest hour. A genuine Sicilian angel. Gabriella. And my soul is briefly resting tonight.

Finally.

The Relationship

We had a brief relation lasting several months. Yes, it was intense and yes, it was passionate, and yes, I brought her back to the states with me, but no, it was not destined to be.

Not in the context of lovers, anyway. In the context of true friendship, that is another story. Gabri is and will always be one of my very best friends.

The problem was mine, not hers.

My hard ways of being a city kid, a lawyer and a warrior proved too much for the fragile relationship to survive. I was a bull in a china shop. I thought, in my know-it-all way, that I could rescue her and that I could save her.

In reality, it was she who rescued me. It was she that saved me. It was she that showed me the way to happiness. I was an idiot and I misplayed the whole thing. Had I known then what I know today, Gabri and I would be together, I think. (Sigh). Such is life.

During those months that we lived together in America she

exposed me to the ways of spirituality, serenity and self-healing. She exposed me to the idea of gentleness. She exposed me to wisdom. I knew nothing. She knew everything.

It was I who became the student, and I learned.

When we returned to Sicily in May of last year, we parted ways in a physical sense, but emotionally I remained attached to her. Our relationship had entered another phase…a mature phase…and I could understand her.

During our talks, she often had made mention of the lack of opportunities for Sicilian graduates for jobs, mostly because many of them were so poor in the English language. Researching the idea while I was with Gabri, I decided to write about it in my next book, *"Gaetano's Trunk"* which I did.

Thus, The Sicilian Project was started directly as a result of my relationship with Gabri. It was she who enlightened me on the topic. It was she that put the idea in my head.

Thus, she influenced me and I in turn influenced those in America who decided to help, and they in turn financially support those in Sicily by educating them.

Thus, Gabri is my hero. She taught me, she influenced me, and she changed my life. And now, she changes the lives of others through the Sicilian Project.

Perhaps the most important thing that she did, for however brief a period of time it was, was to show me that I could in fact love someone again, and that if I wanted that love to be permanent, I had to listen to the other.

Thus, I heard that ping in my heart thanks to Gabri.

Gabri moved to America earlier this year. I will not disclose the location to you. We keep in touch and she is happy. She is working and has decided to get her American equivalency educational credits and perhaps be a doctor in the states.

Thus, I will continue her work in Sicily.

Gabriella, you see, is still my teacher.

Chapter Fourteen

Staring Down the Bad Guy

A. Prologue:

Just because I am an American-Sicilian living in Sicily shouldn't give any native Sicilian crook carte blanche to try to rip me off.

Quite the opposite.

I am a street kid from Lawrence, Massachusetts and have written the book on spotting rip-off artists.

When you live in a rough and tumble city like my hometown, you either eat or be eaten, and I have learned the lessons of the street well. Add in an athletic background and also that of a bare knuckled litigator, and I am not chopped liver, if you know what I mean.

Usually when I travel, I travel alone. The road trips that I took with Vita being the sole exceptions.

When I run about town, or when I run about the countryside, however, I keep to myself. I feel most comfortable this way. I guess you can say that I am a lone wolf.

I always have had the same demeanor when I am in a foreign place as well. I call it the "keep away from me" look. It probably is a defensive mechanism that I have developed over the years, but I have found that it creates less problems this way.

On the other hand, when I am with friends, my persona changes and I am downright friendly.

I usually wear sunglasses when I travel alone. I do this obviously to shield my eyes from the sun, but the dark aviator glasses that I wear have another purpose; I want no one reading my eyes. Especially in a foreign place.

Long ago I learned that the eyes tell the story about a person, not the words that come out of the mouth and I do not want to tip my hand…ever.

One look, a simple look, lays the foundation for any and all communication or potential confrontation. Thus, the best defense for me, developed over many years, is my reading a situation and in a split second reacting to what I see.

When I was a kid, I also developed another defense mechanism… my famous "Zappala Death Stare."

I used to think that if I could put my Death Stare in a bottle, then little old men and old ladies would be able to buy it and be completely safe walking anywhere and at anytime and have no fear anyplace in any city. My patented stare consisted of me slowly lifting my glasses up onto my forehead, establishing contact with whomever I wanted to drill at the moment, and then boring into their eyeballs with my thousand yard death stare until their soul explodes.

As a lawyer, my Death Stare had won me many a battle BEFORE the battle even began. Over time I used to think that maybe I should register it or something, just like Bruce Lee had to register his hands as lethal weapons.

In any case, one stare-down usually did it.

Every so often, someone would actually challenge my stare, but that led to step two; squaring my shoulders and facing the person head on, face to face.

This technique was used on only the hardest of souls, however. Usually my stare coupled with my physical persona had won many a fight before any blows were thrown, which was exactly what Sun Tzu, in his ancient military tactics book *The Art Of War*, said it should be.

You win the battle BEFORE you draw your bow and arrow, he taught.

Now that I have told you about this famous tactic of mine, I will tell you now the story about the day that the salmon was on sale at the market.

B. Staring Down The Bad Guy

Over the last few years, more and more supermarkets in Sicily have been opening up fish departments that have all sorts of fresh fish, delivered by fisherman every day. Huge counters of crushed ice are topped with whatever was caught the night before by local fishermen.

Honestly, there are so many varieties of fish in Sicily that are sold every day I could not possibly name them all for you.

The basic fish, however, are all there every day; sword fish, mackerel, tuna, ten or fifteen varieties of white fish in all sizes and shapes, eel, sardines, "masculinu" — those small fish about 5 inches long that you would grill with a little oil and are the staple of Sicilian Cuisine, all sorts of clams, squid, calamari…you get the picture.

Usually the fish counter is over-flowing with the day's catch, and the earlier you get to the market, the more of a variety you have to pick from. For sure, by one o'clock in the afternoon, the only things left are the mangy looking offerings, so getting there by nine a.m. is crucial.

Which I did on this one particular day. I went to my favorite market to buy fish and to see what they had.

To my surprise, there was a sign that said "Norwegian Salmon fillets 6.60 euro a kilo."

That meant two point two pounds of salmon fillets for about fourteen dollars. Less than seven dollars a pound!

I was excited and wanted to buy a half-kilo. That meant that for a little less than seven dollars, I could buy a pound of salmon, and my mouth was already watering as I pictured myself cooking these babies. With my Sicilian marinade that I'm an expert at making, and some veggies and a salad, I would feast this night for a pittance.

My marinade is a classic Sicilian marinade called "sarmurigghiu". It consists of a garlic clove, added to the juice of four lemons, along with extra virgin olive oil, salt, pepper, and then chopped fresh parsley.

The secret was cooking the fish with as little oil as possible.

In Sicily they have these "fish pans" which have raised ridges on them. The pans are placed on a stove and then the fire is turned on until it gets hot. Then the fish is put on the hot pan. AFTER the fish is cooked, it is placed in the marinade.

In America, we marinade the fish first, and then cook it. In Sicily, they do it in reverse. I much prefer the Sicilian way.

I also use a toaster oven instead of a fish pan, as I prefer the broiling effect better than the pan effect. I simply put the setting on broil and I use a THIN coat of olive oil for all fish I cook, and for salmon, I cook it exactly seven minutes on each side.

After the first five minutes I check the salmon to make sure that the center is moist. Once it is cooked, I place the fish in the marinade for a couple minutes, and then enjoy my feast.

I also line my broiler pan with aluminum foil so there is no messy clean-up. This technique can be used for all sorts of fish. Just adjust the time per the thickness of the fish. Over time, you will be proficient.

In any case, getting back to my story…

So I order a half kilo and the fish guy, a really menacing guy if I ever saw one, glares at me. He gave me the tough guy "take what I give you and be thankful look" that bullies give to people. My radar immediately went up to full operating mode. This bully has picked on the wrong guy to get tough with, and he was about to be taught a lesson direct from Lawrence, Massachusetts.

The fish guy was short, dark and had about three days growth on his face. He looked like a text book tough guy. A thug. I expected to see a pistol sticking out of his waist band, to be truthful with you.

In any event, he put two nice pieces of salmon on the scale as I requested and then he put on the scale about eight ounces of …fish head …useless, non-edible fish head!

I looked at the guy, and realizing that he was about to cheat me, I said to him in broken Sicilian "What are you doing? I don't want any fish head. Take it out of there. I am not paying for a fish head that I cannot eat!"

He looked at me and said "Everybody has to eat," meaning that he was overcharging me so he could pocket some extra money.

Now, I know that when a person usually buys fish at a market and you ask to have it cleaned, the fish is weighed before it is cleaned… just like in the states. This, however, was not the case. Here we have a bunch of salmon fillets all cut up. This guy was trying to pull a fast one.

Well, I flipped my glasses up, established eye contact with him and gave him my patented Zappala Death Stare.

"If you don't take it out now" I said, "there will be two heads on that scale very soon."

I figured what the heck. This guy was clearly trying to rip me off. I was born on a Tuesday, but not last Tuesday.

He turned white. The bully turned white.

He sheepishly said to me "Everybody gets a piece of head in with the fish. That is the way it is."

I looked at him and said "I am counting to three…uno, due…"

At "due", he blinked. The blood drained from his face. He removed the head from my box.

I flipped my glasses back down and de-activated the Death Stare.

"That wasn't so bad, now, was it?" I said. "Remember my face...I will be back again." Then I smiled at him and continued my shopping.

Several other customers saw what I had done, and I was later told that others complained to the manager about him unjustly putting fish heads in with the fillets.

However, in this day and age, this type of nonsense does not fly with me and must stop forever. Consumers simply have to stop getting ripped off.

Thus, the first use of the Zappala Death Stare in Sicily was successfully deployed. I am sure that it may have to be used again sometime, just as it is sometimes used in the states.

By the way, the salmon was exquisite. Norwegian salmon from the cold waters of Norway just melts in your mouth.

When I went back to shop a couple weeks later, the fish guy was nowhere to be found. I was told they had a problem with him and sent him to another store.

No one was any longer putting fish heads on the scale, and I felt good about that.

Score one for the little guy!

Chapter Fifteen

Lisa and Terri: Figlie dell' Etna

Meet Lisa and Terri, two "Figlie dell' Etna" or daughters of Etna. Born in America yet their hearts will always be on a small hillside village near Etna.

This is their story.

Last year, we put together our annual trip to Sicily for our newsletter and Facebook friends. We have organized trips for about seven years, and people always have a lot of fun and experience wonderful memories. Because of the poor economy, last year's group was smaller than usual, but that meant that much more for them to enjoy.

We had made arrangements for them to stay at the Hilton in Naxos and had various day tours planned for them as well including Taormina, Etna, and Messina and all the usual places that visitors would normally go on an organized trip. There were also two days free that people could explore on their own, relax by the hotel pool or hire a private a guide to take them wherever they wanted to go. One couple wanted to go to the Tindari area, and they were accompanied by Gabriella who acted as guide and translator for them.

Two sisters, however, wanted to go to Trecastagni and this story is about them and that special day.

This is a story about Lisa and Terri and family, and memories, and love.

Meet Lisa and Terri

Lisa Dzioba of Salem, New Hampshire and Terri Bamford of West Melbourne Florida are as close as two sisters can possibly be. Both are moms with grown children and are the point in their lives that they can think about themselves a bit. Lisa is the oldest of three sisters and Terri is the youngest.

The fact that they live fifteen hundred miles apart does not faze them one bit. They talk on the phone every day, have the same interests. They love to "junk", which is the art of finding something like a piece of old furniture and completely restoring it. The artistic ability of both ladies turn discarded items into unbelievably beautiful objects of art. Both ladies have enormous creative talent. Lisa used to tell me "We love to turn trash into treasures, Alfred."

Both women are extremely artistic, creative, and a joy to be around. When I first met them, I knew they were very special people, and on this particular side trip, I wanted to be with them as an observer. They had already traveled to Catania once with Gabriella, to meet their relatives Anna, Remigia, Nella, Giuseppina and Pippo and this would be the second meeting with them.

The first meeting had been very emotional, and this meeting would be in Trecastagni, the ancestral home town.

To give a little background on the ladies, they were born and brought up in the immigrant city of Lawrence, Massachusetts, my birth city and home to tens of thousands Sicilian immigrants who flocked to America in the early twentieth century seeking a better life for themselves.

They were brought up on Chestnut Street in Lawrence, an ethnic neighborhood full of Italians, Lebanese, Portuguese, Lithuanians, Syrians, and French Canadian immigrants. They lived in the Italian alcove in that district along with other Sicilian families.

They were very close to their mom's parents, Pasqualina and Salvatore Longo. As a matter of fact, they lived with them for many years. The grandparents instilled in them a profound love for Sicily, Trecastagni, and the patron saints of that community, Saints Alfio, Filadelfo and Cirino, three young brothers martyred by the Romans for their Christian beliefs many centuries ago.

Lisa and Terri's grandfather Salvatore ("Sam") was born in Trecastagni and moved to the states when he was seventeen. Interestingly enough, of the six other siblings in Sam's family, three of his brothers were named Alfio, Filadelfo and Cirino just like the patron saints of Trecastagni.

Not only that, but two of them had also re-located to Lawrence and took part in the annual Feast of the Three Saints Festival which had been started in the early twentieth century by the immigrants from Trecastagni, Viagrande, Pedara, and Sant'Alfio. Thus, both women were steeped in Sicilian culture as children and the love for Sicily was part of their persona.

For me, the coincidences were amazing. Like Sam, both of my grandfathers lived in Trecastagni, like Sam, my grandfathers came to Lawrence as teenagers, and like Sam, my grandfathers worked with their hands and had a profound love for the Three Saints. I really wanted to go with them on this day. The stars seemed to be aligning for reasons that I did not know.

Both Lisa and Terri saw how hard their grandfather worked. He was a mason and a skilled craftsman in the building art, skills which legions of Sicilians excelled, and he also had a back yard garden in Lawrence with a vegetable and a flower garden, four fig trees and a peach tree!

Having four fig trees in New England is no easy chore. Each fall, the trees must be covered and buried in the soil in order to prevent frost damage, and dug up and re-planted every spring. To do this every year with four trees was truly a labor of love.

Their grandmother Pasqualina (called "Lena" by everyone) was the homemaker, filling the house with the flavors and textures of the old world. She was born in Rhode Island but her parents were from Catania, and she too had been instilled with a deep love of Sicily. Despite the fact that both now lived in Massachusetts, neither grandparent forgot Sicily and tried their hardest…often under trying conditions…to maintain a small piece of heaven on Chestnut Street in Lawrence for their family.

Lena not only was an excellent cook but she was an excellent teacher too. She taught both Lisa and Terri to cook exquisite Sicilian food. Lisa told me once that she regrets not learning to crochet from Lena as Lena was also talented in that department. Terri did, however, and crochets to this day. As nanas often do…the girls have fond memories of Lena's love and warmth and they both lovingly remember "curling" their grandmother's hair as they spent quiet time together.

Thus, these were the images of Sicily that were burned into the memories of Lisa and Terri and which had compelled them to make this trip to Sicily. This trip was a life long dream for both.

The story that I am describing to you is not a new one; rather it had been played out hundreds of thousands of times over the twentieth century, and chances are that if you're reading this story something similar happened to you or to your family.

Sicilians came and settled the cities of Lawrence, Boston, New York City, New Haven, Philadelphia, Chicago, New Orleans and countless other cities and their story is all the same; some of them never forgot Sicily. Some instilled into their children a love for their new homeland whole some of them instilled in their children and grandchildren a love for the ancestral homeland. Thus, Lisa's story and Terri's story has a common background perhaps with your story too.

What is amazing is that I never met these two wonderful women while I lived in Lawrence. Thus, you could imagine my surprise when they first asked if I could make arrangements to get a guide and to take them to their ancestral village of Trecastagni, which is MY ancestral village!

It seemed the stars were aligning for a very special day indeed.

As Lisa and Terri had married, raised families, and grew into adulthood, their life long wish of going to Sicily never died. Their dream was this trip, and this day was the apex of that dream.

Gabriella and I were privileged to observe it, too. Both of us will always be thankful for that.

So, when they heard about my little Sicilian trip, they signed up quickly and asked me to arrange this side trip for them.

Gabriella (or Gabri as I call her, my friend from the previous chapter) often did translation work for me in Sicily or taught Italian to my students who were interested, or she acted as a guide and escort for my clients who needed help. The four of us…me, Gabri, Lisa and Terri set off in my trusty Fiat Punto and headed from Naxos to Trecastagni one sunny October morning last fall.

The ride from Naxos to Trecastagni was a splash of magic that day. The sun was brilliant and the countryside burst with the color, sounds and beauty of Sicilian splendor. The hillside towns around Etna have a special aura that cannot be adequately described. Suffice it to say that the ride to Trecastagni was simply a very wonderful experience for the ladies.

We zipped down the autostrada for about fourteen kilometers and then exited at Acireale. Trecastagni is a small village on the south west side of Etna and we began the ascent…driving up past Valverde, then Viagrande, then Monte Russo…and finally into Trecastagni.

Trecastagni is beautiful in the fall; actually it's beautiful all year around. The summer villas owned by northerners dot the hillside. In summer, people escape here to avoid the hot cities of the north. Etna's breezes comfort them. The town is aglow on this day with flowers, palm trees and fruit stands. It is remarkably clean for a Sicilian town.

Truly a picture-post card village. My village. Our village.

Gabri had already taken the women to Trecastagni to try find family records and then to Catania to meet their family for a joyous re-union two days previously. Gabri told me about the hugs, tears, smiles and laughter she witnessed. Gabri told me that she was moved to tears herself.

Today we were here to hunt down their ancestral home, see the Church of Sant'Alfio, go to the cemetery to try to find the grave of their great-grandmother, and finally, go to their cousin Gaetano's farmhouse and have lunch.. Gabri told me that the family had put out a huge spread of food for them on the first visit, so I was eagerly looking forward to lunch!

We arrived in Trecastagni, and parked the car. We were at the right place, Piazza Marconi, the beautiful center of town next to the municipal offices.

A huge contingent of family members was there to greet us. At least ten of them, all hugging and kissing the women at the same time and the two women returned each hug and kiss as if it were their last. I thought to myself as I witnessed this reunion the beauty of familial love that it was strikingly evident that there was an abundance of love on everyone's part.

Our first stop was the Church of Sant'Alfio. We entered this solemn and sacred place and the women were in awe as I pointed out things to them. Lisa was especially impressed with the area in the church where believers would carry votive candles during the feast and take them to be offered in this place. Terri loved the Hall of Miracles; a series of rooms where people who had prayed to the saints and had their prayers answered had drawn pictures in tribute to their intercessions. The hall contained thousands of such pictures.

Our next task was to locate the ancestral home.

All we had for information was that it was located next to the old jail. Asking around, we quickly found the old jail which was no more than one hundred and fifty yards from MY old ancestral home. On a sleepy side street, close to my family home and the jail we located Lisa and Terri's ancestral home. Can you believe it? Their ancestral home was literally around the corner from my ancestral home!

Everyone got chills watching the two women looking at the house. Tears flowed. Pictures were taken. A silence enveloped the group as people became introspective about the event they were experiencing. It was a remarkable moment. The area was quiet, solemn and peaceful and it seemed like the spirits of their ancestors were waiting for us to visit them.

We the piled in our cars and headed to the cemetery which was not too far away. We were looking for the grave of their great grandmother. Lisa's and Terri's family had told them that it was impossible to find the grave as it was so old, and that they had already tried locating the grave but were unsuccessful.

Undaunted, the ladies wanted to go and see for themselves.

It was Terri who located the grave. There was a marker on the ground with no gravestone. The name was clear as day. Terri had found her great-grandmother's grave!

Something compelling had pushed Terri to look where she did and it called out to her.

Looking around to make note of the location so that the next time they visit we could easily find it, I was stunned to find it located almost next to the Zappala grave!

Thus, a confluence of time, coincidence and events had led me on this day to see their ancestral house located right around the corner for my ancestral house, and now finding a grave of my ancestor as well.

To finish off a magical afternoon, we then went to their cousin Gaetano's farmhouse for lunch. The house was located on the outskirts of Trecastagni, away from the downtown traffic. It had a huge kitchen and a magnificent yard with all kinds of fig, olive, lemon and orange trees. The place was beautiful, roomy and comfortable.

As you can imagine, the family spared no expense for their

American relatives. Food overflowed the table. We ate, and we ate, and then we ate some more. After lunch, old pictures were pulled out from drawers, new pictures taken and Gabri was going a mile a minute translating everything for the women. What a scene. Seventy-five years of history getting caught up in a two-hour span by this family.

Looking at Gabri, I could tell she was enjoying herself. This wasn't her job on this day. Instead, it had turned out to be a journey of discovery and Gabri loved every second of it. She later told me it was one of the best days for her in a long time.

On the ride back to the hotel that afternoon, both women told us that this day was one of the happiest days of their lives. Both women vowed to return to Sicily soon and they would be in communication with their blood relatives more frequently now.

Lisa, Terri and Gabri are Facebook friends, and Lisa and I communicate very frequently too. A special bond was formed on that trip, I think.

What I am most happy about is this; last week, Lisa received her Italian passport. She has become an Italian citizen! Terri had done all the research and Lisa had done all the running around and five months after the trip she was notified that everything was in order. Terri has an appointment at the Italian Consulate's office in Miami soon and by the time this book is published will also have her Italian passport too.

Thus both women will complete the circle started by their grandfather and grandmother.

As for me, I could not be happier or more privileged to know these remarkable women. I hope that one day soon we can journey back to Trecastagni for another re-union.

This was truly a special day with special people.

Chapter Sixteen

Places

1. The Fountain of Arethusa- The Ortygia Section of Siracusa.

I have written about one of my favorite cities in Sicily, Siracusa, in the past. This ancient, compact and lovely sea-side city today speaks of its illustrious past only through its bustling tourist trade on the island of Ortygia, founded by the ancient Corinthians almost twenty-two hundred years ago.

In *Gaetano's Trunk*, I wrote about the tyrant Gelone and his impact on Western civilization that was truly profound. I wrote that if Gelone had not defeated the Phoenicians in a huge battle and slaughtered tens of thousands of them, they might have later re-enforced the invading Persian army in Greece. Thus, Siracusa has an important part in Western civilization history today.

The major street leading into Ortygia is named after him. While there are plenty of historic sites there for you to enjoy in Siracusa including the wonderful Greek Theater, my favorite spot is a little known fresh water fountain that leads into the sea. It doesn't even look like a fountain; rather it looks like a cement duck pond.

This is the Fountain of Arethusa and if you have a creative streak in you to write, paint or create things, put this place in your bucket list of places to visit.

Arethusa, according to Greek legend, was a nymph and a lover of Artemis. One day, while she was bathing in the river Alpheus, the river fell in love with her and wanted her for itself. In order to protect her, Artemis turned her into a fresh water spring which flowed beneath the river, emerging in a small area in Ortygia…today know as the Fountain of Arethusa, and out to the sea.

This is quite a place. It resembles a duck pond with walls and is ringed with papyrus plants. It has been a source of inspiration for those in the creative arts for centuries. Every day scores of visitors ring the little fountain in a very contemplative manner.

I make it a point to stroll down to the fountain every time I visit Ortygia and I always learn something a little extra about the Greek lore here too. Of course, I always stroll to the Duomo and the enormous piazza Duomo to have an espresso and granite, but this little spot is my favorite in Siracusa.

Put the Fountain of Arethusa on your list of places to visit. It is a treasure.

2. Messina, The Duomo, The Campanile (The clock tower), The Port

Whenever I get down in the dumps, I hop in my car and zip forty-five minutes north on the autostrada and head into Messina. When I need to get inspired by a people who just would never give up, Messina is where I go.

Not that Messina is extraordinarily beautiful; it is not. How can it be?

Over ninety percent of the city was destroyed in the Second World War, not to mention the enormously destructive earthquake of 1908 that killed tens of thousands of inhabitants and flattened the city.

The one-two punch of a devastating earthquake and then unrelenting Allied bombing less than forty years later would kill the spirit of the most hearty.

But not those from Messina.

I go there not for its natural beauty but rather to get my soul refreshed and to remember that "never say die" attitude that the people of this city have long maintained. They are survivors pure and simple.

A casual glance at the history of this place is a story of siege, destruction, domination, occupation, disaster, yet also one of constant re-birth.

I love the port of Messina. This is usually my first stop every time I visit the city.

I park my car and walk to the water's edge. The port has been central to the city's history since it founding millennia ago. It has been a point of entry for invaders since time immemorial.

I think of the Crusader ships as they departed from this gathering point on their way to the Holy Land during the Crusade Period. I can almost visualize the Crusader insignia on the departing ships, and the insignias of all the kings, knights, man servants, and legions of foot soldiers that loaded onto the wooden ships from this point in order to free the Holy Land.

Their spirit still lingers. I can still feel it when I gaze into the sea from the port.

As does the spirit of uncounted thousands who perished during the earthquake of 1908 while heading for the waters edge as they desperately tried to save themselves. Many emotions grip me as I gaze into the sea. For me, Messina is a very special and sacred place.

I always visit the Duomo and say a prayer for the souls of the departed when I am in town. As I sit in this dark yet beautiful Cathedral, I realize that it was repeatedly destroyed over the centuries as well. Only a very small portion of the original twelfth century Church remains today. The rest of it was destroyed in the 1908 earthquake and subsequently damaged again during the Second World War.

I always enjoy the daily show by the huge mechanical clock in the Campanile or tower immediately adjacent to the Cathedral. It is a modern contrivance, built in the 1930s. It was built by a German company and at over 180 feet high is considered one of the world's biggest clock towers, if not the biggest.

The intricate mechanical figures that pop out in a tight sequence… a giant lion…a golden cock…the statues of Dina and Clarenza…two heroines' of the people who led an insurrection back in the thirteenth century…Gospel scenes…you name it…are a spectacle indeed.

Virtually every tour operator in Sicily includes this location on the trip itinerary, so during the summer season it takes on a touristic ambiance. In the winter it is a much more contemplative place as the hordes of tourists are gone.

There are many other areas to explore in one of my favorite cities, but one last thing I will tell you is that there is no finer pastry that the pastry of Messina. If you love to eat sweet things, welcome to heaven!

On the way out of town, I always treat myself to something delicious usually a pastry filled with their delicious boiled creams and covered with heavenly icings… and make a mental note to return as soon as I can.

Messina... the Port…the Duomo…its rich history…the spirit of its people…put this one on your bucket list of places to see as well!

3. Castellammare del Golfo

In my opinion, I would match the views from both Castellammare del Golfo and from Taormina with any other two other European sights. They are perhaps the two most spectacular vistas in Europe. One is on the east coast, the other on the west coast. They are many miles apart but incite the same feeling of awe and inspiration to any who visit these places.

Earlier in the book, I wrote about stopping in Castellammare del Golfo with Vita on the way to San Vito lo Capo. The panoramic view from the highway is something that a visitor to Sicily should not miss. However, traveling down below to the ancient port and its surroundings is equally as beautiful and you should take the time to do this. It will be well worth your while.

The ancient port speaks of ancient populations that once thrived here. Many people from many nations, invaders all, made this a point of embarkation for wheat and other raw materials for generations. Many things departed Sicily from this port. Very few things, however, were delivered here.

To protect the port an ancient castle stands guard. Built perhaps by the Arabs or the Normans, it reminds us of the strategic import of this port. Many died protecting this place.

Traveling the streets of the port, I was amazed by the natural beauty of the coastline. I was reminded how dependant the people here are on the sea to this day. Grain transports have now been replaced with small fishing boats and pleasure craft of every variety. Unfortunately, the economic downturn has hit this area very hard, and many boats are docked or out of the water waiting patiently to be called again back to the sea.

My friend Manfredi Barbera from the famed Palermitan olive oil company Manfredi Barbera & Figli took me to this area for the first time many years ago. I have returned since countless times to gaze at the sea and its calm waters.

There is constant discussion as to which side of the island, east or west, north or south, is the most beautiful. I know this, if I were a painter, the view from the highway would be my water lilies. As Monet spent a career painting his water lilies, I would spend a career painting this panorama.

If you do stop into the area, be sure to visit the Duomo in town and the castle…and stop and try the local fare at any local restaurant… the fish that you will eat was probably in the nearby sea hours earlier.

Another place to put on your list!

4. Pachino, Portopalo, Marzamemi and Capo Passero

According to legend Capo Passero…on the southeastern tip of Sicily where I am going to tell you about, along with Capo Boeo on the western side of the island and Capo Peloro near Messina, constitute…according to ancient lore…the three points of the island that was originally called "Trinacria"…three capes. If you locate the three Capes or Capos on a map of Sicily….North, South, and West…you will get the rough outline shape of the outline of Sicily.

Or so the story goes.

If you look at a map of Sicily, Pachino, Portopalo, Marzamemi, and Capo Passero are located near the tip of southeastern Sicily and are accessible only by a two lane highway from land.

There is no superhighway to take you there directly. As they say in Maine "You can't get there from here!"

The ride from Siracusa due south is a pleasant one. As you pass through Avola you will see Noto off to the distance. The landscape is completely different in this part of Sicily, becoming increasingly hot and arid the further south you drive.

I bought my first place back in the late 1990s in Pachino and remember only a few things about the place. One thing I remember is that there was the huge bee hive that I wrote about in a previous book. It was the biggest bee hive I had ever seen in my life there. Another thing I remembered was that the best fish restaurant that I ever ate in my life was located in Portopalo. I also remembered how hot…furnace hot…it was in the month of August.

Now let me tell you briefly some other reasons that this area is great enough for you to make the trek into this part of Sicily. They flat out have Europe's best tasting tomatoes (the small cherry tomatoes as we call them), and their melons are so sweet they literally melt in your mouth. In other words Pachino is the home to the best fruits and vegetables in Sicily.

Pachino is also known also being a fishing mecca, and the small town of Portopalo has a really great fish market where the fishermen auction off their catch every day to restaurant and hotel operators and fish markets from all over. I spent an enjoyable morning one day watching the action at the market here. It was fast and furious.

Great fishing is one attraction, and the friendly people who seen to have a distinct Arabic background are another. The white sand beach was awesome, not like the pebble beaches located everywhere else, and I remember that my place was 100 yards from the water. These are the things I remember about Pachino.

Did I tell you that the wine is great too? Or that the cauliflower is almost a foot and a half wide? Did I tell you that the herbs from this area are the island's best? Did I tell you the most important thing… that this is God's country, plain and simple? Yes it is…truly.

Yes, Pachino is off the beaten tract and it certainly is not a tourist attraction, for sure. However, northern Italians know of Pachino, and gobble up their tomatoes and vegetables and fruit like there is no tomorrow. And, in the summer they flock to rent the beach houses that dot the coastline.

I remember that when we first went to Pachino to locate my new house my dear friend Rosario Messina had little info as to where the house was located. All we had was a photo of the house somewhere near a lighthouse and that was it.

I had purchased the house from the estate of an American and that was pretty much all the information I had going into the deal…a photo of a house on a white sand beach, located by a lighthouse… yet we were able to find the house thanks to Rosario's great sense of direction.

The house was abandoned and stripped down by thieves, but we lovingly restored it over time and for years enjoyed the area, especially the restaurants that featured prawns, calamari, sea urchin, vongole, and all sorts of small tuna and white fish.

God…my mouth waters now thinking of all those meals!

Back in the states, probably the nicest people that I know are the Cautedella family. My friend Joe Cautedella had a very successful funeral business in the Merrimack Valley area and his daughter

Amber has a radio talk program. Many others from my hometown originally were from this area and settled in the Gloucester area of Massachusetts to fish and also in New Orleans where they became great shrimp fishermen...just like Forest Gump!

Back in the days when Libya was America's enemy, the rumor around town was that the Americans CIA had listening posts here to keep track of the dictator Gaddafi. Libya is located just a stone's throw off the coast...did you know that?

In any case, the southeastern tip of Sicily is a great out of the place that you will love as you travel around Sicily.

Pachino...I just love the place!

5. Sciacca- The Ceramic and the Food

Everyone knows that Caltanissetta and Santo Stefano di Camastra have wonderful ceramic shops but did you know that same was true in the ancient and beautiful port town of Sciacca?

People in Sicily know all about the spas, thermal springs and mud baths of Sciacca. For many years Italians and Europeans have frequented the spas in the area surrounding Sciacca.

The mud baths are legendary.

People also know that the port of Sciacca nestled below the town is a great place to buy fish every day from the fishermen who fish the surrounding sea. It is also a good place to dine in one of the great fish restaurants that are nestled here and there on the side streets. Did you know that the ceramic work on the steps leading here and there and the ceramic work on houses on virtually every corner of the town is simply astounding?

I bet people also don't know that the town has a great Duomo and that the old part of Sciacca features a truly great little osteria, Osteria Cappellino di Salvino Cottone, on via Cappellino no. 24. It is wondrous to behold.

This tiny hole in the wall restaurant has no menu and the owner simply prepares food and serves it. The wine is simply terrific too. I can still taste all the great things he prepared for Vita and I on our road trip there earlier in the summer as I researched materials for this book.

Another interesting thing that I think you do not know was that the famous black and white Italian film "Seduced and Abandoned" filmed in the 1950s was filmed in the center of town.

Many people come to Sciacca for many reasons. My friend Jeanne Scaduto Belmonte from East Boston and the famous entertainer Pat Benti from Revere Massachusetts both trace their origins here, as does the famous former middleweight champion Tony DiMarco. All have roots that they can trace back to this great little village.

Like the fishermen from Pachino, many from Sciacca immigrated to America and brought with them the famous feast of San Gennaro, the Fisherman's Feast, celebrated in Boston's North End and other places every year.

I bet you did not know that this gem of a little town has tens of thousands American-Sicilians yearning for the day that they can visit this place. To them it would fulfill a life long ambition.

If you didn't know all these things…now you do! This one also belongs on your list of places in Sicily to visit.

Chapter Seventeen

Tony DeMarco- The Sicilian Kid Who Made Good

Tony DeMarco is a friend of mine, and he is one of my heroes.

He is an even better friend of my brother Tom Zappala and his wife Ellen Zappala. They love the man so much that Ellen wrote a book about this son of immigrants from Sciacca. I am pleased to say that a lot of people have read the book and now know the man.

Tony DeMarco is one of the most famous and beloved athletes from Boston, Massachusetts. He is still called "The Champ" when he strolls through his old North End neighborhood, Boston's Little Italy.

Meet Tony DeMarco…"Nardo"…who was once the undisputed Welterweight Champion of the boxing world. He is a Sicilian-American who has made us all proud.

He was born Leonardo Liotta to Vincenzo and Giacomina Liotta, immigrants from Sciacca. Little "Nardo" grew up on Fleet Street in the Italian working class section of Boston, the North End. His father, Vincenzo, was a cobbler by trade who worked long hours to support his four growing children. He always encouraged Nardo's interest in boxing, but probably never imagined that his son would someday become the undisputed Welterweight Champion of the World.

Nardo learned to fight on the streets of Boston and in the local Boys Club. He quickly figured out that he had a special talent as a puncher, often defeating boys much older than himself. At the young age of 15, Nardo was ready to box as an amateur, but was not old enough to qualify for a boxing license.

Not wanting to wait three years to get started in the ring, Nardo borrowed the name Tony DeMarco from a boyhood friend who was 18 years old, and from that point on he boxed under the name Tony DeMarco. Tony's pro career began on October 21, 1948 when he KO'd Meteor Jones in the first round. He then began to work his way up the ladder beating opponents such as Vic Young, Bobby Weaver, Manny Santos and Pug Brown.

Over the first two years of his career, he jumped out to a quick

10-1 record knocking out 8 opponents. After he started working with Sammy Fuller as his trainer and well-known manager Rip Valenti, his level of competition improved and he fought more seasoned boxers like Pat Demers, Chick Boucher, and Teddy "Red Top" Davis. With an impressive 30-3 record at this point in his career, Tony became known for his devastating punching power.

He finally gained national recognition when he beat Lightweight Champion Paddy DeMarco, Wilbur Wilson, contender George Arujo, and Lightweight Champ Jimmy Carter.

Tony got his chance at the crown early in 1955 when he signed to take on Welterweight Champion Johnny Saxton for the undisputed Welterweight Championship of the World. The fight was scheduled to take place on April 1, 1955 at the famed Boston Garden, just a few blocks from the Liotta home on Fleet Street.

The entire city of Boston was in a state of frenzy because this local boy could possibly win the championship right in his own neighborhood. The young twenty-three year old Sicilian kid from the neighborhood was taking on the Champ.

The fight was a furious battle from the start. In the 14th round Tony decked Saxton and was then in control. He proceeded to hit the Champ with twenty-four consecutive punches before the referee stopped the fight.

The crowd at the Garden went crazy. Tony was Champion of the World.

People poured onto the streets of Boston to celebrate. In fact, Italians throughout Massachusetts celebrated for many days. Tony became an instant celebrity, appearing with politicians, sports personalities, and entertainers all over the country. Three months later, he had to defend his title against the "Onion Farmer" from New York, Carmen Basilio.

He moved his training camp to the Catskills where he became close friends with the great heavyweight champion from Brockton, Massachusetts and fellow Italian, Rocky Marciano.

In what is considered one of the greatest matches of all time, DeMarco and Basilio battered each other for 12 furious rounds. Tony lost to Carmen on cuts in the 12th in one of the closest matches in boxing history. A rematch was quickly scheduled. After eight brutal rounds Tony had Carmen on the ropes, but the tide turned and Basilio retained the championship by knocking out Tony in the 12th round. This fight was voted the Fight of the Decade and is still considered one of the top 10 greatest fights of all time.

Tony's story does not end there. He went on to fight a total of 8 world champions over his great career. In 1956 he fought Bud Smith, Kid Gavilan, and Gaspar Ortega. That year he also fought Vince Martinez at historic Fenway Park. Although he fought in many venues, Tony was a favorite at the Boston Garden. He holds the record for most fights and most sellouts at the Boston Garden.

Besides the moments of triumph during his professional life, there were also moments of tragedy that forever shaped his life. Tony lost a brother, a son and a daughter all at very young ages, but he learned from those losses.

Today, Tony DeMarco is still very active in the greater Boston community and in the boxing world. He attends many charity events, mentors young boxers and is one of the sport's greatest supporters. He is President Emeritus of the Massachusetts Chapter of the National Italian American Sports Hall of Fame, and recently published his autobiography entitled, *Nardo: Memoirs of a Boxing Champion.* In recognition of Tony, the city of Boston renamed the upper end of Fleet Street in the North End to Tony DeMarco Way, and in October 2012 during Italian Heritage month, a statue of Tony DeMarco was placed at the Gateway to the North End.

Fiercely proud of both his Sicilian heritage and his boxing heritage, Tony DeMarco is a true Boston icon. You can read all about Tony too on his web site www.tkotony.com.

Tony DeMarco. I am glad that he came into the life of Tom and Ellen. He is a great man and has a great story to tell.

Chapter Eighteen

The Taxi Men of Naxos

The men of Naxos work long hours for little money and they sacrifice everything for their families.

They are simple hard-working men. They are the Taxi Men of Naxos and they are my friends. And now, much like what is happening all over the European Union, things are tough for them, very tough.

They wait and they hope that things will improve, and they do this stoically, bravely. Patiently they sit by their gleaming white taxis… and wait.

This is especially so now during La Crisi, the economic crisis that has engulfed the world and that nearly brought Sicily to her knees. With the unemployment rate over 50% for college grads and nearly 20% for everyone else, folks feel fortunate enough just to have a job.

It doesn't matter if are getting paid, just so long as they have something to do with their lives. That they have something that gives them hope and the opportunity of maybe getting paid. That is what's important. But more importantly, if you are fortunate enough to have a paying job, no matter how small the pay may be, the last thing you want to do is to quit that job—even if you make little or no money.

Somehow, Sicilians manage to cobble together a month's salary in this harsh economic environment. Nationally, the average monthly salary is about 1450 euro a month, equivalent to less than $2000 USD a month. Oftentimes, this has to feed a family of four, five, six or more.

The Taxi Men of Naxos are perfect examples of the sacrifice that Sicilians are making right now in an attempt to provide, however meager, for their families. If they are fortunate, their spouses are working as this helps enormously with the economic problems facing the family. However, jobs are scarce right now. Historically, driving a taxi has been a man's job in Sicily.

So, their gleaming white taxis sit and they wait…sometimes all day…for a fare or two, and sometime a whole day goes by with no fare at all.

Still, they wait.

One thing about these men, and many are my friends, is that they never complain about the situation. Why should they? Complaining is a waste of energy, and everyone right now is in the same boat. Somehow, they survive, just as their forefathers survived other hardships.

The Taxi Men of Naxos…a mirror of what is going on in Sicily today.

Every major tourist area has reserved parking spots located close to major hotels that are lined with taxis. In New York City cabbies can roam the streets looking for a fare. In Italy, and particularly in Sicily the chaos is highly structured. As a taxi man, you have an assigned location, and that one location is where you sit and wait for a fare… even if it never comes.

In Naxos, the spot is right across the street from the Hilton Hotel. And there are other spots by other hotels too, but this is the spot that I have observed for years.

Pools of twelve to fourteen drivers share the same eight reserved spots seven days a week. Twelve to fourteen families provided for by a stretch of roadway no more than eight car lengths long. They rotate their time on these spaces throughout the day.

Usually, the fares want to go to places like the airport to catch a return flight home, or to Taormina where they can sight see or shop, or perhaps to visit a relative nearby.

If the taxi man has to travel to the airport, a distance of roughly twenty-two miles, he is fortunate if he finds a return fare back to Naxos. At the airport, cabs are everywhere. In Taormina, the spots also are highly restricted, and sometimes they are able to get a return fare back to Naxos.

The ebb and flow of a taxi man's life is constant uncertainty with the job; the uncertainty of getting a fare or a return fare: the uncertainty of what tomorrow will bring or not bring; the uncertainty of surviving in this economy. Still, they persevere. And they do so with dignity.

When you are a Taxi Man, you do not need to wear a watch. A Taxi Man works seven days a week from roughly 11am in the morning until 2 or 3 am the following day with only a few hours off in the afternoon for a bite to eat and to spend a little time with the family.

If you are lucky enough to book a return fare to Fontanarossa

Airport in Catania, then your day will start at 4:30 am, because flights from Catania to Rome begin at 6am, and that is the way of the business.

In Sicily, the tourist season stretches out for perhaps nine months a year, with five of those months being decent income months for the Taxi Men, and the other four months not so decent. And then there are two or three months with barely any work at all while they wait for the tourists to return.

These men usually do not own their taxis. They usually work for a company and like cab companies everywhere they pay a fee usually to rent the taxi plus expenses like paying for gasoline…which means that high petrol cost very much hurt their business. This past summer, due to the increase in petrol in Italy, what used to be a ten euro ride from Naxos to Taormina became a fifteen euro ride, and unhappy tourists took the increased fees out on the taxi men. Tips slowly disappeared.

My friends Nunzio and Carmelo are brothers and taxi men in Naxos. I make it a point to visit them every time I go to Café Sikelia to visit Roberto. In between fares, they play Sicilian card games like "Scopa" or "Settee mensu", or engage in conversation with their colleagues. They try to keep their minds busy as the day wears on. Sometimes, time takes forever to pass, especially on those hot Sicilian afternoons.

Both Nunzio and Carmelo are married with little children and both work eighty hours a week for their uncle Alfio, who also drives a taxi. They never complain about a thing, just the opposite as a matter of fact. They are cheerful and friendly and never fail to give me a big hug as a greeting. Like all the Taxi Men, they refuse to give up and refuse to quit on life. They are an excellent source of inspiration for me and maybe for you too.

The Taxi Men of Naxos: Pietro Lombardo, Antonio Franco (and his 10 year old son Alessio who helps his father drive his taxi. Alessio is 10 years old!), Nunzio Priolo, Carmelo Priolo, Alfio Priolo, Antonio Lenoci, Antonio Ponturo, Lino Ieni, Mario Pennisi, Seby (Sebastiano) Melita, Cosmo-Alfio Restivo, Vincenzo Franco.

The Taxi Men of Naxos. If you see them in Naxos, please tell them that Alfred sends his respect.

Chapter Nineteen

Zucchini Heaven

I had no idea that zucchini was such a healthy food. No wonder it is a staple of Sicilian cuisine! I used to think that zucchini was just something that mom put on the pasta for color and was something that I had to push away in order to get to the pasta every night when I was kid.

What an idiot.

In Sicily, I eat pasta no more than twice a week. When I do eat pasta, I eat it for lunch and try to have a modest serving, not the huge serving that we Americans eat. Ideally, I eat no more than 100 grams for lunch. Sometimes I cheat a little and eat maybe 125 grams, which is still a lot less that the amount that I would eat in America. In the olden days of reckless eating in America, I would cook a pound of pasta (roughly 500 grams give or take) for two people and always have a second helping. Now, I eat half that amount…and never have seconds.

I have learned to substitute organic brown rice and even couscous a couple times a week for pasta. I have also found that most of the recipes that I use for pasta dishes can easily be adapted to both of these other carbohydrate offerings as well.

Couscous tastes especially good with some kind of a broth… maybe fish stock…on the side as well.

In any case, today I will pay homage to the magical and healthful zucchini.

In Sicily (and in America for that matter), these wondrous creations of nature take many forms, flavors and textures. Green zucchini, white zucchini, yellow zucchini, zucchini florets, small zucchini, long zucchini, thick zucchini, skinny zucchini…it really makes no difference.

No matter how you make zucchini, over pasta, or as a side dish, or with tomato, or grilled, the list is endless. What is important to know is that these treasures of nature have many health benefits . This is an added attraction. They are healthy and plentiful here in Sicily and I have really explored all the ways that they can be prepared.

For millennia, Sicilians have eaten zucchini in all the above forms because anyone with half a brain can grow them. Plant the seed, water them and poof...several weeks later you have a million of them coming out of your ears!

They are cheap, plentiful, delicious...and incredibly healthy for you too.

How is a zucchini healthy, you may ask? Well, according to the United States Food and Drug Administration, one cup of zucchini has less than 40 calories and has 10% of your daily fiber, and can help maintain low blood sugar too. Eating zucchini instead of something with more calories in it helps the diet too. It fills you up, taste delicious and has vitamins and minerals that help keep other organs healthy.

For me it is very important now that I am older to watch what I eat because I must have a genetic pre-disposition to high cholesterol according to my doctor, and I must watch what I eat very carefully the older I get. My doctor told me that it is good for me to eat zucchini every day as it will help me lower my blood pressure.

For me, if I can get away from taking a pill for this problem, I am "all ears" as they say.

I also was surprised to learn that zucchini has high levels of both vitamins C and vitamin A, and these vitamins help my blood vessels fight off hardening of the arteries. The fiber contained in zucchini also helps fight cancer since it promotes a healthy colon. Not only that, but the phytonutrients found in zucchini help reduce the benign conditions in which the prostrate gland can enlarge. It also helps fight arthritis, asthma, and rheumatoid arthritis.

For me, when I was researching the health effects of zucchini I was also surprised to learn that a cup of zucchini contains 10% of the daily requirement of magnesium , a mineral that helps prevent heart attack and stroke! Most importantly to a big guy like me who has a problem with high blood pressure, the potassium found in zucchini helps fight high blood pressure. Thus, this vegetable is vastly underrated as a healthy food alternative, in my opinion.

I am not an expert in health foods by any means but I spent many hours on various web sites researching the health benefits of zucchini and came away convinced that I will eat more of these "heath bullets" and try them in as many different combinations as well. Maybe a zucchini a day will keep the doctor away too!

Coupled with drinking two glasses of red wine (the health

benefits of drinking two small glasses of red wine are just now being recognized) and also drinking plenty of water every day means that it has been over two years now since I last purchased a bottle of soda pop. I feel better about myself; I think my health has improved just by making small changes in what I eat. I have concluded that I can control the quality of my life a bit now, and plan on doing exactly that.

I think that people mistakenly believe that zucchini has to be fried in order to be flavorful. I never deep fry anything anymore. As a matter of fact, you can make zucchini taste wonderful using only two or three tablespoons of extra virgin oil ...and that will be enough for you to make at least four servings!

Of course, they can be sliced and grilled too, steamed, boiled, stuffed...but here is my favorite way to eat zucchini and pasta.

Maybe you will enjoy this!

Alfred's Simple Zucchini and Pasta Dish

As always, I usually pour myself a glass of red wine while I prepare my food. I do this for two reasons: first, it "puts me in the mood' so to speak, and second, there is something about a glass of red wine that "opens the senses" to the flavors and textures of the food you are preparing.

At the market, I selected four zucchini, each about average size. I have also purchased some freshly made pasta (something about one to one and a half inches long...straight, squiggly...whatever you like. If you are using dry pasta, a rigatoni works nice here). I also have some freshly grated Parmesan cheese, and a good quality extra virgin olive oil, some salt and pepper too. If you like a tangy taste, you can add in red pepper flakes too.

In a skillet with a cover, I put no more than 2 to 3 tablespoons of extra virgin olive oil and put the fire on low. The object here is not to fry the zucchini. The object is to soften the zucchini and cook them a little to release their flavor. Make sure you have a cover for your skillet too. The steam will help soften the zucchini.

Cut the zucchini into slices about ¼ of an inch thick. Not too thin, not too thick. Keep the skin on too! Just slice them. Then put the zucchini in the pan, add a little salt and pepper and put the lid on.

Every five minutes or so, with a wooden spoon, turn them and moved them around. If you want a tangy flavor, add in the red pepper flakes now too. After about 15 minutes, they will be done. Stick a fork in one piece. It should not be soggy. It should be soft, not soggy. Then shut the fire off. Keep the lid on.

Meanwhile, in another pan, you have started to boil the water for the pasta. Always use a good size pan. Add your salt in when the water is boiling, and then add in the pasta.

The secret here is that you want the pasta to be cooked very al dente. That means you need to keep an eye on the pasta. That is why the wine you are drinking is important! You will be interested in the pasta you are cooking because your senses are alive.

When the past is at the *al dente* stage literally.... "to the teeth" in Italian...the stage when the pasta is still firm and not over cooked... take out of the pasta pan a cup of the pasta water and put it aside. Use a ladle to do this.

After you have done this, strain the pasta with a colander, add in some extra virgin oil, then place the pasta back into the pan and put it back on to a medium fire. Now add in the water from the pasta that you have reserved.

When the water comes to a boil again ...this will take no more than a minute or two... add in the entire pan of zucchini...drippings and all, and cook for another three minutes. Stir with a wooden spoon but be careful not to break the softened zucchini.

In three minutes, turn the heat off.

When you serve the pasta and zucchini, you can top with Parmesan cheese. Some people like to add a little more extra virgin olive oil too, and a little more black pepper.

If you have made a red sauce (note that my recipe has no sauce in it!), this whole thing works well with a red sauce too.

Simply add the zucchini into the red sauce before you mix it into the pasta!

Red sauce or no red sauce... the important thing is that you get to know the zucchini, and my way will maybe inspire you to try one of the many thousands of other ways to eat this healthy and glorious gift from nature!

Enjoy!

Chapter Twenty

A Very Enjoyable Road Trip Indeed
The Return of Vita
Caltagirone, Ragusa, Modica... and Everything Else in Between

Prologue:

When Vita left to work in Greece in June, and as you can imagine, I was feeling a little down in the dumps.

Not because we had a huge love affair or anything like that, but because on my last road trip I had connected with her in a way that had solved a lot of emotional questions that had lingered in my head for over a decade. She had become one of my best friends. I missed her terribly.

To make matters worse, I did not know if I was going to see her again. Her work plans called for her to be assigned to Greece, then Spain, then the Dolomites…not Sicily.

Emails and texts are fine to keep tabs on one another, but there is nothing like face to face contact, sharing space so to speak. While we sent emails back and forth, the Magic Carpet patiently waited for her return. It had purred like a kitten when we had traveled together, and it longed for the day that it would happen again.

No matter what I did…car washes…new tires…new windshield blades…an oil change…nothing seemed to lift the Magic Carpet out of its doldrums. It missed Vita too.

I knew she was busy in Greece with Lithuanian tourists and I also knew that in her off time she probably was doing something of an athletic nature such as scuba diving, hiking, parasailing or something. The beautiful Greek island of Rhodes offered her the perfect place to do these sorts of activities. Still, I missed her.

Last I had heard from her was that after the assignment in Greece she would head either to Spain for the winter or to the Italian Dolomites, I was resigned to the fact that I probably would not see her again for another year.

My creative juices were left for wanting, that's for sure.

Thus, for a variety of reasons I was disappointed. I was disappointed because she was my travel companion who knew the Sicilian countryside and helped make it come alive, and she was an excellent navigator to boot. With her as a co-pilot, I knew that we would always get to our destination. Remember when we travelled together we never took main roads. For us, Sicily was always back roads. That is how we rolled.

"Vita, the sun shines less brightly and the colors are not as brilliant here since you left," I once complained in an email. "Maybe you can come back and we can do another road-trip?" I would often ask.

Never a reply to that question though.

While my new book was progressing nicely, and the goings on of The Sicilian Project were keeping me very busy, as was acting as host two nights a week at Roberto's place in Naxos for visiting Americans, (I had somehow now become the "author in residence" there and lots of folks came on these nights to talk with me and Roberto), something was missing.

There was a hole in my heart, and that hole was called "Vita".

She was my friend and had taught me a lot and I missed her. And my book needed her too. I had painted a nice picture with her on our other trips. The Mona Lisa was complete…except the head still hadn't been painted. I need her to complete the picture.

Then one day in September I received a text from her.

"I am returning to Sicily for five weeks. Not too happy about it," she texted.

Maybe she wasn't too happy about it, but I was thrilled.

Seems that her company had re-assigned her due to the economic crisis, and she was returning to Sicily to work with Lithuanian and Russian tourists that were here for the fall season. She loved Rhodes and the barbeques that she had there with her friends, and while I am sure that she loved Sicily too, the sudden re-assignment surprised her.

In any case, in mid-September, out of the blue, she returned.

When I saw her for the first time at Roberto's' place the next day, I sensed that she was genuinely happy to see me again. I know I was happy to see her.

Her big blue eyes twinkled as we greeted each other and with that infectious and beautiful smile of hers it seemed that the saying that "distance doesn't affect a friendship" is true. We picked up where our friendship had left off and immediately I could feel my creative juices beginning to stir again.

Over dinner a couple of days later, I asked her if she would be willing to do another road trip with me. She told me her schedule was jammed packed, but she would see what she could do. "No promises, Alfred," she said, "maybe."

This was a good enough answer for me. I waited. And I hoped.

Several days later, she sent me another text. "I have a little time off. Want to go to Caltagirone, Ragusa and Modica and explore the area for a day? I can meet you at 8:00 a.m. tomorrow."

"Sure" I replied. Of course, I was elated, but that was my answer to her. I could have said "Yippie!" or "Hooray!" or "Excellent!" but the Bostonian in me kept it simple. All I knew was that I was hitting the road again with Vita.

We were going to explore a section of Sicily that I always wanted to investigate, and with Vita as my co-pilot, I knew that I could accomplish more with her in fifteen hours than I could with anyone else in three days.

At exactly 8:00 am the following day, I picked her up in Naxos at Roberto's place in the Magic Carpet, my 2000 blue Fiat Punto with 249,000 kilometers on it, or *ferro vecchio* (old iron) as some one called it. It was as happy as I was that Vita would again be my side-kick for this day. It was happy, I swear.

I had a full tank of gas, money in my pocket, Vita as a sidekick and Sicily to explore...what else could a guy ask for?

A. Paradiso...a Great and Visual Experience

The plan today was to head down the autostrada until we got past Catania, and pick up Route 417 south and a little west and head into Caltagirone—a ninety minute ride with no traffic. Since had we left early, we managed to clear Greater Catania morning rush hour traffic with no problem and south of Catania we exited onto Route 417.

This road is a standard two lane road, and is notorious for garbage and debris left on the side road by locals. It is also place where prostitutes lounge on chairs and wait for passing truckers to ply their trade.

This ten-mile stretch is an embarrassment to Sicily. I often complain bitterly to everyone who would listen about this, but I also knew that as soon as we cleared this section....about a ten mile stretch... the natural beauty of the scenery would begin to dominate at we leave the grime of Catania behind.

I was correct. Within minutes my Sicily re-immerged and I felt relieved. I made a mental note though, to complain again to the authorities. I knew that if I did that I would just be whistling in the wind. Some things never change. It is called corruption.

About twenty kilometers out of Catania, driving past the plains and farm land, the vegetation, colors, smells, and textures all took on an artistic tone. It was like we had entered a different planet.

Thankfully.

We passed a small three-wheeled truck loaded with yellow melons and we slowed the car just enough for Vita to get a great shot of the little truck. It was great how the driver...who noticed that we were photographing his vehicle...broke into a broad grin and gave us a huge wave hello. The image that she took was a great one too. I later posted it on my blog.

As we got deeper into the southern portion of the roadway, fico d'india trees or cactus pear trees loaded with "prickly pears" or "cactus pears" appeared on both sides of the road. We stopped the car to take several interesting shots of these delectable delights. This is the harvest time for prickly pears and the trees were just loaded with them. The rich red color contrasted sharply with the green cactus background and the colors popped at us. Persimmons also are harvested at this time of the year, as are mushrooms, musk melons, chestnuts, and purple cauliflower.

Further down the road, the Sicilian farmland teemed with orange and lemon trees, olive groves, and many other types of vegetables, especially leafy ones like purple cauliflower and broccoli. This are was rich and fertile...thanks to the gifts from Etna. And the perfume of the Sicilian air makes it seem like paradise to me.

The area of Route 412 between Ramacca to the north and Patagonia to the south, a stretch of roadway roughly fifty kilometers long and devoid of people and villages, reminded me of a surrealistic dream image of beauty and bounty.

Getting closer to Caltagirone, we passed briefly through Acate, Grammichele and Niscemi......in order to get a feel for the area. On out last trip together, we had been on the other side by the sea and had stayed overnight in Gela, so this was an interesting juxtaposition of land and terrain.

My trusty Magic Carpet was in a particularly good mood this early morning and hummed along the roadway. We had Otmar Liebart's *Luna Negra* on the iPod and the flamingo music fit the occasion perfectly. The Magic Carpet was aloft and fully operational, and as usual, little was spoken between Vita and I.

Both of us were too busy absorbing the visuals that were hitting our senses. One stretch of roadway was so overgrown with vegetation that the tops of the trees from one side of the road were nearly touching the tops of the trees from the other side of the road. Thus, for a few kilometers we experienced a surreal tunnel-like effect of the Sicilian countryside.

I made a mental note of this stretch of roadway, but I also made another one that the next time I traveled down this area, I would completely by-pass the grungy start of the roadway back in Catania and cut across the country further down the line.

In the distance, after a spectacular drive that was an experience in and of itself, loomed the magical and beautiful town of Caltagirone... which neither of us had ever visited.

Both of us peered ahead in eager anticipation.

B. Caltagirone

I had heard many stories over the years about this beautiful place. Set high atop a huge incline, the city presented itself in a staggering and beautiful panoramic vision. Since the cloudy day had cleared up and the sun was now brightly shining, we were able to get some breathtaking images with the camera as we approached the city.

We had the barest of knowledge of Caltagirone going in....I knew that it (along with most of Messina, Noto, Ragusa, Modica and Catania and about five hundred other small villages) had been devastated in the earthquake of 1693, and that it has emerged from the ruins as a beautiful baroque city and had established itself as a center of some of Sicily's finest pottery makers as well.

I also knew that Caltagirone was not huge, a population of less than 45,000 living on the hills of the town. It was a picture book setting in all its resplendent glory. While we were still in the province of Catania, we were over 70 kilometers away from the city and nothing else reminded me of Catania.

This place was flat out beautiful and I thought vastly underrated as a tourist destination.

We also knew about the "stairs." Everyone in Sicily knows about the "stairs." Officially known as the *Staircase of Santa Maria del Monte*, it is a 142-step staircase leading to the Church of Santa Maria del Monte. Each step decorated on each riser with a different ceramic decoration. It was a tourist mecca of the first magnitude. Vita and I were going to find these steps and climb them.

Finding them was the first order of business.

Since we knew that the historical section was high on a hill, we just kept heading up hill. Finally, I stopped the car and asked for directions to the stairs. We were surprised to learn that we were headed in the right direction. In no time, we had located the area, found a great parking spot and headed to the stairs.

The street leading to the stairs is a great area by the way…very clean, picturesque and full of little shops, coffee bars, and quaint piazzas and impeccably neat and clean.

Finially…ahead of us…right after a small piazza…we found the stairs. Not only are they incredibly beautiful to look at, they were indeed formidable! One hundred and forty two steps, they looked like one thousand and forty two steps to me. And we were going to climb them!

As we began our ascent up the steps, I thought of how beautiful this place must be every July 25th on the feast of the city's patron Saint James, when candles are placed on every step up to the church at the top of the stairway. Next July 25th I shall return, I thought to myself.

I was surprised to find many ceramic shops on each side as we climbed the steps too…and also entrances to apartments where people lived!

I could not believe that people would climb these steps every day. How do they bring their groceries up, I wondered? In any case,

Vita tackled the steps as an athlete would, just walk up the steps one and a time. Me? I walked up one step then horizontally walked the length of the step and climbed the next step…and horizontally walk the step again …until I made it to the top. For me, this was an easy trek up the steps.

Surprisingly, I was not out of breathe and in excellent shape when I made it to the top.

We asked another couple who were following us up the steps to take a photo of us as proof that we indeed "climbed the steps" of this magnificent place.

At the top of the steps was the *Church of Santa Maria del Monte…* we both wandered about the church and I was amazed at the statuary there.

On the way down we decided to take a side road from the top down and we were glad that we did. The tiny streets that we wandered about were profoundly picturesque, narrow, cobble-stoned and just very special. Neither Vita nor I spoke as we took in the lovely sights and sounds of Caltagirone's back streets.

Hitting the bottom of the street, we found a great little pastry shop and sampled Castiglione's legendary pastry. I had perhaps the best cornetti that I ever ate. Vita had a ricotta cornetti and I had a vanilla boiled cream cornetti. The pastry crust was just superb and along with a cappuccino, it was just what the doctor ordered! By the way, I grabbed a napkin with the address of this pastry shop or "bar" as they are called here. The name is Judica & Trieste e Figli 22 Via Principe Amedeo in Caltagirone. When in town this is a "must visit."

As we head for the car, we both glanced at each other. We knew that we would return to this special place, and soon, too. By the way, if you want to see what I have written about so far, the website *http://www.comune.caltagirone.ct.it/comune.caltagirone.ct.it* will give you a glance at where you have just been with us.

C. Off to Donnafugata

We always travel the back roads of Sicily.

As two experienced travelers, we have confidence in our ability to find our way around, especially since we have excellent maps to guide us. We decided to take an "off the beaten track" approach to get to Ragusa. It was a very round about way as we wanted to see the countryside of the southeastern portion of Sicily. We decided that we would first detour to Donnafugata and see the famous castle there.

We agreed to work our way south until we got to Vittoria and then head to Donnafugata before heading to Ragusa. We immediately picked up the indications to Vittoria as we left town and headed on a series of minor roadways through beautiful Sicilian countryside on this splendid fall day.

The sun had broken through and we were awash with brilliant sunshine. Through village after village we meandered slowly…stopping frequently to admire the landscape, or a vista, or a farm or anything scenic really. Two friends in a beat up old jalopy accompanied only by The Gypsy Kings, Bob Markey and the French singer Patricia Kaas. Again silence was the order of the day.

Vita is not the type of woman to make small talk. Most of her communication (with me at least) is visual. As she told me a million times "Alfred, I know who you are"…and she is correct. Every once in a while, as we were working our way through Santa Maria dell'Idria or San Pietro or Acate or the sleepy town of Casazza, and between sweeping agricultural sights and textures, we would talk about her homeland, Lithuania, and life there both pre and post Soviet Union fall, and what she wanted to do with her life. Mostly though, we observed, looked and enjoyed.

I obviously had grown very attached to this woman…a respect for a woman wise beyond her years, and I really wanted to know what made her tick. She always was very are tight lipped and every so often a morsel that she would drop here and there helped me understand what made her the woman she is. The setting was perfect for small and intermittent conversation, but we both let the scenery do the talking for us.

After an hour drive through the remarkable country, we hit the grid-like city of Vittoria, and neither of us was impressed with the sterile environment we found in the criss-cross pattern of a town. We both decided that next time in the area we would eliminate this town completely from out itinerary and headed out of town as fast as we could.

We pushed further south to Donnafugata.

The first thing we noticed was the scenery began to change…a lot. Sweeping vistas and farmlands were replaced with stone walls… everywhere it seemed, and carob trees. The landscape took on a Spanish flavor. I felt at times that I was driving through Mexico and that Zorro would come riding by and jump over one of these walls. Plots of land were everywhere. To me they looked like share-cropper parcels separated by three to four foot high walls with light colored brown-yellow stones. It was a stark change of pace from what we had been seeing.

After a thirty-minute drive, we found the tiny resort castle of Donnafugata. However, when we arrived, the castle was closed. We decided to nose around in any case and took pictures of the exterior of the castle and talked to local townspeople.

Talking to an old timer that was in a nearby bar, I found that the castle originally was an Arab fortification and was a source for fresh water. The castle was later destroyed and sometime in the 17th century was re-built by a Spanish baron who gave it its distinct Spanish flair. The surrounding area was quiet and animals such as goats and cows, fenced in penned areas, created quite a nice ambiance to the town.

The castle, named Castello di Donnafugata, is opened to the public for tours every day except Mondays. There is also a golf course nearby (one of only three in all of Sicily), and the wine from this area is outstanding as well we were told. It is a very pretty and picturesque place and worth a comeback visit someday.

After wandering around a bit more, we decided to push on to Ragusa…about twenty kilometers to the east, and see what was happening there.

So far, the road trip was happening exactly as planned…relaxing, fun, and educational. As I drove on the road to Ragusa, I was thinking how fortunate that the universe had placed me in this place at this time with this person, and was grateful for the opportunity to experience these things.

I resolved to try to paint a picture as accurately as possible for those who would never get here …for them as well as for me.

D. Ragusa Iblea

Ragusa is not a small town. It is a busy city of over 75,000 people and is the provincial capital of the province of Ragusa. If you have not been to this section of Sicily, circle this place on the map and make place to spend one full day here…preferably two full days.

The city is located high on a hill, which offered a natural defenses long ago against invaders. The panoramic view of the city as we approached it was a photographer's delight. It is almost impossible to take a bad picture of the outline of Ragusa as it is approached, and Vita was able to capture magnificent images as I drove up the enormous hill to the city.

From what I gathered the night before in my lightening quick background check of the area, many different people originally occupied the area…Greeks, Carthaginians, Romans, Byzantines, Arabs, Normans and Spanish. All took their hand at occupying the land stretching back over two millennia and the diverse cultures fused together to create a place so special that I will certainly return here time and again just to educate myself further.

The devastating earthquake of 1693, which wiped out most of Messina, Catania, and hundreds of small villages in the north and east portion of Sicily also hit this area hard. Thousands were killed, but as is the case with the resilient Sicilians, the town was re-built.

Since our time here was limited, we focused only on one of the two major areas of Ragusa, Ragusa Iblea. We would leave the other higher area Ragusa Superior accessible by a series of bridges until our next visit. That meant that we would not see the main monument, *The Cathedral of San Giovanni Battista* (Saint John the Baptist…the city's patron saint), which was fine with us, as our main goal on this day was to walk the street of Ibla and examine the texture and architecture of this place.

We were very fortunate as we arrived. We found a great parking place next to the *Church of "Le Anime del Purgatorio"*, The Church of the Souls of Purgatory, and knew that we were centrally located. We would spend several hours walking the entire area, and since it had stopped raining and the sun shining brightly, we were delighted to take advantage of the break in the weather.

I was overwhelmed at the statuary in this church, and spent several extra minutes looking at these museum quality pieces.

Outside several elderly men were sitting and I chatted with them for a while. They suggested that we see the old area and pointed the way. That is exactly what we did.

We proceeded up about a quarter mile until the road split, and we chose the cobble-stoned path as opposed to the asphalt road. We were led into the 16th to 17th century old section, lined with small houses and tiny side stairways leading to who knows where. This section had been destroyed during the earthquake, but had been re-built over the centuries since. As I walked the cobble-stoned narrow street, I was reminded of Boston's North End .I also was reminded of Taormina without the sea, with the many step passageways. I was staggered to see the closed and damaged Church of Santa Lucia built in 1561… that's early 16th century…with most of its facade still intact.

Drifting up one stairway, we finally hit the main tourist are of Iblea…the baroque and magnificent Cathedral of San Giorgio area …built in the 18th century.

Time and time again as we wandered the area around the Public Gardens and the many streets and ways attached to this district, the array of churches and cathedrals, the many spectacular homes, and the overwhelming beauty of this area staggered us. This was Baroque architecture at its finest.

We wandered this area for three hours, logging at least ten kilometers on foot. We were silent most of the time, communicating with eye contact or head nods…there was really no need for chit chat at this moment. We were both lost in the beauty of this place.

On the way back to the car, I was convinced that we had lost our way. One street began to blend into another, and even though I have an excellent sense of direction, in the morass of back alleys and side streets, I had lost my orientation. I questioned Vita and suggested that maybe we should back pedal to a major street and then re-orientate ourselves a bit. Trouble was, she wasn't lost. Her sense of direction was even better than mine, and within 100 yards, we had located the car.

Her sly smile said it all.

By this time, we were both starving but decided to wait until we drove the short distance to Modica before we got a bite to eat.

As we left Iblea, I made an oath to myself that I will return to see the other section…and soon. This road trip had now surpassed my expectations…and we still had one more place to visit.

E. Modica

I did not know much about Modica prior to our brief visit there. The day was getting late and we were hungry and a little tired, but we decided to push on and spend a few hours in this magnificent Baroque city.

I knew that the famous writer, and Nobel Prize winner (1959) in Literature, Salvatore Quasimodo was born here. I also knew that the chocolate of Modica is legendary in Sicily, as are the carob products, wine, and olive oils too. I knew that many great small to medium size hotels and tourist places are located here, but really not much else.

I found out about its storied past and how it was once a terrific cultural and educational center. The story of Modica is a story of a rich and cultural city with a legendary past I learned, and I wanted to see it.

No matter what I learned about Modica, I can tell you this, the people of this splendid city of 40,000 are truly friendly, generous, helpful and genuinely interested in hearing what you have to say.

Of all the assets that Modica has to offer, in my opinion, her people are at the top of the list.

After the short drive from Ragusa and by now really wanting something to eat, we were able to find a spot to park on the main street within walking distance of the *Cathedral of Saint Giorgio*…the major church and Duomo in Modica. This area is filled with shops, outdoor cafés and gift shops, and most importantly, shops that sell the famed chocolate and also the famed gelato of Modica, reputed among the best in Sicily.

By the time we arrived, the restaurants were not yet opened (it was 6 p.m. in the evening and the restaurants open later). We decided to head to a bar and see what we could find there. In any case, we knew that we would treat ourselves to a gelato at least if we could not find anything to eat.

Walking into a quaint little bar, we immediately sensed that the offerings there would be above average. At this time of day, the arancini, pizza, calzone and the like that sit under glass cases in bars can be dried out and cold. However, this particular place was humming with activity, as this was the main place in the area that sold food until the restaurants opened. The offerings were hot, delicious, flavorful, and filling. I chose something that looked like a folded up pizza (without the sauce) that has cheese, sausage and spinach inside. It was outstanding. Vita had a vegetable offering similar to mine without the meat.

Surprisingly, we both blurted out that we wanted beer (Moretti) with our food when asked what we wanted to drink. The combination of a cold beer and the hot and delicious food after walking so much in Ragusa Ibla restored our energy.

We spent fifteen minutes talking with the two owners who turned out to have relatives in New York. Their big smiles and conversation topped off a very pleasant interlude. Now refreshed, it was now time to explore a little and find some (a) gelato and (b) chocolate.

As we admired the many buildings during our brief walking expedition, I asked a passer-by where we could find an excellent chocolate shop as well as an excellent gelateria. He directed us to the area of the *Duomo of San Giorgio* and suggested two places that we should visit.

We weaved our way in and out many shops before finally admiring the spectacular *Duomo of San Giorgio* ...a wonderful testament to those people who rebuilt the cathedral after the earthquake of 1693. The baroque character of the Duomo was simply breathtaking to see.

I again made a mental note to return to Modica soon and do a more thorough examination of all the churches and architectural wonders of this magnificent city, but we were getting pressed for time and had to push on.

We found the best chocolate shop in town and Vita's eyes widened as we entered. Chocolate making is a major industry in Modica...and the shop had a great representative sampling of what was made in Modica and most of it was on display and for sale. It was almost like the Sicilian version of Hershey, Pennsylvania in terms of displaying what the town made. I also found out later that you could even tour the factory down the road that makes the chocolate if you make arrangements beforehand.

Be advised, however, that the chocolate here is not the milk chocolate variety of commercial American manufacturers. It is dark, grainy chocolate and the American pallet may not be used to the taste. Plus, there are different flavorings beside just plain old chocolate flavor. Most importantly, at this particular shop we were able to taste morsels of each flavor before selecting several to buy. Now it was time for dessert, and we headed to the gelateria.

I can tell you this much, nowhere in Sicily have I tasted such wonderful gelato as in Modica. If there was a competition for Sicily's best gelato, I would award Modica first prize! I choose among the many offerings two flavors to try, ricotta gelato and pistachio gelato. As I write this sentence I can still taste the heavenly flavors of those two delights. Vita had two flavors as well, tiramisu and cinnamon (highly unusual) and the look on her face as she gobbled them down told me that she was also enjoying every morsel of her treat too.

After wandering around a bit more after our reward for the day, we decided to head back to Naxos. It was getting late and we had traveled far and wide on this day. We had a ninety-minute trip back and the day already had stretched out to a twelve-hour day.

The trip back to Naxos was again a pleasurable experience in the Magic Carpet, despite our exhaustion. As we listened to the music that was playing at day's end…soft and contemplative music by Paul Schwartz...and enveloped by our own individual thoughts as we drove through the darkened Sicilian countryside at night, both of us were lost in our own world.

At one point, Vita asked me "Alfred, what are you thinking about?" I look at her and said "Nothing, really."

However, what I was thinking about was how fortunate I was that I had a companion such as Vita to share these experiences with me. After she had left for Greece, a few others had volunteered to be my travel companion on these road trips, but truth be told, I only wanted to travel with Vita.

Our friendship had grown over the summer months and was now a deep and mutual friendship. I remember that someone told me one time that people can go through life and count with one hand how many true friends they have. If that is the case, then Vita would be counted in my handful of true friends, and I am glad that she was my sidekick today. I also thought to myself that I would like to do one more road trip with her before she had to leave again. Don't push it, I thought to myself. Be happy with what you have.

Postscript:

Several days later, I bumped into Vita at Roberto's. Her big smile and hug told me that she was genuinely happy to see me. "Alfred," she said," I think I can make another trip with you. Do you want to go someplace again next week? I have a little free time." "Sure" I said.

And then I smiled inside.

Chapter Twenty-One

The Sicilian Project Revisited

Last year when *Gaetano's Trunk* was published, I wrote a chapter about what I considered to be Sicily's biggest economic problem: the lack of enough English-speaking Sicilians to compete in the world markets.

In my book, I complained about the overall lack of excellent English courses that are offered to students, and wistfully called for the creation of The Sicilian Project, which would dedicate itself to the teaching of English in Sicily paid for by the largess of Americans of Sicilian descent. While there are many excellent teachers of English in Sicily, I mused, there simply are not enough to make the island competitive with the rest of the European Union and the world.

At the time, I said that America has been good to the Sicilian immigrants who came to her shores seeking a better way of life, and since there were double the amount of Sicilian-Americans (approximately twelve million Americans claim Sicilian ancestry) than there are people living in Sicily (the population of Sicily is five and a half million), then maybe we as Americans can do something about this problem.

Guess what?

We have.

While the Sicilian Project was only a dream in my mind's eye when I wrote that chapter last year, today I am pleased to say that we are up and operational, that students are being taught English in Sicily, and that while there is a long way to go...we are off to the races!

This past year, we raised money, are now a duly registered Massachusetts non-profit corporation with an outstanding Board of Directors and we are in the process of getting the Internal Revenue to recognize us as a 501-(C) 3 non-profit (which we hope will happen soon).

And, what is the most important part of all?

We have started educating Sicilian youngsters in English ... roughly 100 by the time you read this book. We also money put aside to educate another fifty as well...with many more (we hope) still to come!

The Sicilian project will educate 100 kids this year and is on its way to helping the young in Sicily! How about that!

Here is the story of what happened since last year, and I am sure that you will smile when you read about it. However, we still need a lot of help, and I am hopeful that one of you (maybe a lot more that one) will step up to the plate and help out!

The Story of the Sicilian Project (So far):

After *Gaetano's Trunk* was published in November of 2011, I embarked on my speaking tour as I had done for my first book, *The Reverse Immigrant.*

The local newspapers where I live in Massachusetts had been doing an excellent job of helping me get the word out about my books, especially Tom Duggan's Valley Patriot in Methuen, Massachusetts. Even though Tommy isn't "Sicilian," I dubbed him an honorary Sicilian because he has tirelessly promoted our mission and everything that we do here in Sicily. I am proud to count him as one of my friends. Rosemary Ford of the Eagle Tribune in North Andover Massachusetts also has printed stories several stories on what we are doing. The Massachusetts Lawyer's Weekly in Boston did a great piece as well. Fra Noi Magazine in Chicago, Radio Station WCCM in Methuen Massachusetts, and a host of other papers nationally published reviews and/or interviews about me and my two books, and The Sicilian Project as well. I consider their efforts vitally important to what we are trying to accomplish here. Collectively, they have helped push the word out to Sicilian Americans and Italian Americans throughout America, and are directly responsible for helping change the lives of people here. I am grateful for all their help…as are the kids here in Sicily.

This time, however, I decided to talk about starting the Sicilian Project during my promotional talks as I figured it was an excellent chance to see if others would be interested in helping me get kids educated in Sicily.

I addressed Rotary Clubs, did book signings at libraries, and appeared on local cable television programs, talking to various groups about Sicily, my books and the Sicilian Project. One day I received an invitation to talk to a group of Sicilian Americans from a social group in Manhattan. Since New York City has the largest concentration of Sicilian Americans in the United States, I quickly accepted the invitation and traveled there to speak to a great group of roughly fifty people hosted by the wonderful and knowledgeable Sicily lovers, Vincent Titone and Karen LaRosa.

Both are friends of mine and are really a credit to their Sicilian roots. Vincent has labored for years promoting Sicily to New Yorkers, and Karen has worked tirelessly working to bring concert singers to Sicily…which she has done several times. I am proud that I can count both as dear friends. This group was simply wonderful to me and to my daughter Catie Rae whom I had brought with me. But, most importantly, it convinced me that the Sicilian Project was something that I really wanted to see get off the ground. Besides talking about it, we were now doing something about it. One way or the other, this thing was going to become a reality.

Soon, I was talking it up in my newsletter. Then I created a page about the Sicilian Project on my website. Here it is: *http://www.alfredzappala.com/sicilianproject.html*. Then I started talking about it on my two Facebook pages and even created a Sicilian project Fan Page: Here it is: https://www.facebook.com/BeYourBestSicilian and really began talking it up far and wide.

One day, I received an email from a gentleman named Steven Carbone from Stowe, Vermont. Steve explained to me in that first email (we now have exchanged countless emails, and have spent time in Sicily together) how much he loved Sicily, especially Taormina, and how he agreed with my philosophy. He also thought that the lack of English speakers was holding Sicily back. He told me that he had family in the area, and had visited Sicily many times…as had his wife and daughter. He asked that I call him to discuss the matter further. He wanted to help.

I promptly called him and we talked. We hit it off immediately. We found that we both had a lot in common. From humble beginnings and non-stop hard work, he had become successful in life. He had become far more successful in life professionally than I could ever dream as a matter of fact. He was a pillar of society in Vermont, heading charitable organizations, professional organizations, and had a distinguished background. Yet, like me, had a very humble beginning in life as the grandson of a Sicilian immigrant. He offered to help.

He told me that he wanted to get the ball rolling, and sure enough, a few days later, I received a substantial check (one of several he has sent) to indeed get the ball rolling.

Elated, I quickly made the appropriate announcements, and all of a sudden small donations began to trickle in on the web site's donation page. Steve had primed the pump and once people saw that this idea was becoming reality, began to get enthusiastic about what we were trying to launch.

Realizing that we now had enough money collected to at least start something in Sicily, I contacted my dear friend Donnamarie Kelly-Pignone who had worked for many years as an international educational expert at Babilonia Language School in Taormina... reputed to be the "Harvard" of language schools in Sicily. Here is the link to their web site: *http://www.babilonia.it/*

She quickly understood what I wanted to do, and after consulting with the school's director and founder Alessandro Adorno, agreed to two hugely important things: (1) That she would act as Director of Curriculum for the Sicilian Project and (2) that Babilonia would serve as our base of operations in Sicily, and that through Babilonia's contacts throughout Sicily, as The Sicilian Project expanded, it would supervise the work of other schools that we found.

Suddenly, we had something going!

Through the grace of God, we had found an angel who got the ball rolling and now an excellent school to implement the dream.

In late June of 2012 we educated our first group of 9 high school students at Babilonia, and currently programs are ongoing there on a regular basis. We have classes now scheduled into 2013! We also started a small program for elementary children in the small mountain village of Viagrande taught by a woman that All Things Sicilian once sponsored in America to learn English. Thus for Maria Pace, the student that we once brought to America to learn English, the circle was complete. She was teaching students in her home town. The first nine students finished a program there as well.

I had the good fortune to visit both locations this summer while classes were progressing and the students were just crazy with joy to meet me and to thank me for the opportunity.

In September of 2012, when Steve Carbone visited Taormina (he is now on our Board of Directors along with Vincent Titone mentioned above), we had a meeting with Alessandro Adorno at Babilonia to plan out future classes. We are convinced that The Sicilian Project will expand greatly as time passes and will also accomplish great things. Already, word is spreading like wildfire about what we are doing.

Three weeks ago, I received an email from a gentleman from Texas…Mr. Giovanni Lanza…who was born in Monreale, on the other side of Sicily, and he offered to provide seed money for an English program to be started there as well. Several days later, a check arrived in the mail. I am now in the process of vetting out a school in that area right now, and shortly we will be educating students in the western part of Sicily, our third location, as well.

Here is the point: Sicily needs your help. So does The Sicilian Project. Sicily was good to our ancestors who came to America seeking a better way of life. If you are reading this book, chances are you are of the exact demographic that I am speaking about, and I am sure that you can help us out. Right now, the economic crisis is bleeding Sicily to death. The unemployment rate for youngsters 16 to 24 years old is over 50%! The young are leaving Sicily in droves. We need to stem the tide.

We need to collectively help Sicily…and we need to do it now. Our goal with The Sicilian project is to double in size this year. We want to educate 200 more students…a modest goal indeed. That mean we will influence 200 lives…maybe more.

You can target a donation if you can provide sufficient seed money. If you cannot do that, then "every bean fills the bag" as they say, so please donate what you can. As quickly as we gather money, we will re-direct it to the teaching of English. This is what we can do.

There are many Mr. Carbones and Mr. Lanzas out there and we need to find them one by one and get Sicily to boot strap itself … quickly.

I am hopeful that by next year, when I write my fourth book on Sicily, that I can report to you even more progress.

However, as the Dalai Lama once said "The journey of a thousand miles starts with the first step."

We have taken the first step by creating something tangible. Now, you must help us…please.

It will warm your heart to do so…I promise.

A small contribution from you will help the Project a great deal!

Chapter Twenty-Two

Bella Figura...Still Completely Foreign to Me

Meet the original anti-bella figura guy. The polar opposite guy, as a matter of fact.

Me.

God, my ancestors must be rolling over in their grave. Having bella figura is so...well...Italian...and I am completely devoid of it? What is bella-figura you ask? Well, that is a tough question to answer and the best way to describe it is to give you several examples.

Note however that the concept is completely foreign to me and the best way for me to describe what it means is to give to you several examples. That might help.

Let me explain that bella figura is really a way of life and applies to just about everything a person in Italy (Sicily) does in life. It is a perception of things. It is a projection of how you want to be perceived. That, I think, fits the concept better.

It applies to many things in Italian and Sicilian life including the way a person dresses, the way a person acts, the way a person thinks and conducts himself. It influences Italian and Sicilian culture tremendously.

You can be out of work, have nothing but lint in your pocket and live with your mother, but if you are dressed elegantly and hold your head high when talking with friends or while walking down the street...then you have it.

On the other hand you can be educated and underdressed for an occasion and drive a car not befitting your status in life (this is me I am describing, by the way). And no...you certainly do not have it!

I see workers well dressed and snappy looking all the time in bright orange or yellow uniforms that are always neat and clean. That's bella figura.

Have you ever seen a really nifty policeman stroll the streets of Boston or New York with a nicely starched shirt and highly creased pants? Some do, to me sure...but it is not a way of life as it is here.

Especially in Sicily. Even the municipal police...the local police...

all look handsome in their uniforms and hold their head high and have their shoulders held back when they walk. That is bella-figura.

Have you ever seen a well dressed man in America with a sport coat elegantly thrown over both of his shoulders on a hot evening as he casually walks by or with a cashmere sweater tied in a little knot and the sweater is elegantly placed over his shoulders?

However, just about on any hot night in any plaza in Sicily after dusk you will see this....as well as elderly men in jackets and ties... even white shirts. That is bella-figura.

Are you beginning to get the picture?

"Bella Figura" literally means "beautiful figure" but what it really means to me is "to give a good impression." Or it could mean to live the life you have, be who you are, do it with dignity and with flare... this concept is what you perceive it to be, I have learned. How you project yourself to people is of paramount importance.

Over time I have learned that the term really is an attitude...and an outlook on life. If you look good, you will logically conduct yourself with elegance and culture. If you conduct yourself with elegance and culture...that is the expected way.

While it really makes a lot of sense to me as I think about it, as an America living in Sicily, I prefer to think and act in the manner that I was taught in America. Dress for yourself and be comfortable, and the hell with everyone thinks.

However, this leads to something not very "bella figura...the perception that perhaps you are arrogant. Here is where the perception of the arrogant American comes from, I think. I guess I am to blame. I just want to be me...as the song goes.

Unfortunately, when in Sicily, I dress, talk, act, think and even drive as an American, but there is good reason for that. My thinking is why should I not be comfortable with all things? Who do I have to impress? Why do I have to impress? If I want to wear a jacket and tie for a meeting in Taormina in ninety-five degree heat without a tie on, what is wrong with that? What is wrong with a nice pair of slacks and a polo shirt, or a nice pair of slacks and an open collar shirt?

Well, to some it does not give bella figura. "You are a lawyer, Alfred", I was told. "You must always dress the part." Huh? Why? Are you nuts? I do not understand…

Earlier this summer, I had a very short-lived relationship with an elegant woman that I met in Taormina. She was beautiful, graceful, smart, independent…really a modern-day Sicilian woman. We had met through a mutual friend, and after several meetings we made plans to go out for dinner for dinner.

I showed up as I normally do when I go out: nice slacks, sports jacket, beautiful shirt…but no tie. Casual but elegant as we call it in the states.

When I picked her up (she was dressed to the nines, by the way), she said to me in Italian as she saw my old beat Fiat Punto automobile "ferro vecchio"…old iron. This means that the way I was dressed and the auto I was driving did not befit my status as an attorney. Maybe I should have shown up in an Armani suit and a Mercedes…but that is not how I roll. I am me and what you see is what you get I told her.

The evening was a disaster for a lot of reasons, including the fact that at some point she told me that she was a communist and that I must be a fascist because of my conservative views.

Here she was an admitted communist, saying this to me, as she was dressed to the nines in Gucci, Prada, and a host of other Italian designer clothes. It was then that I understood, even a communist must have bella-figura. I wondered if one communist would say to the other upon greeting each other "Ciao Mario…great Armani suit you have on, comrade." I stupidly asked her that question too, which was not very bella figura.

To me, it just didn't fit. Neither did the relationship, which quickly died.

Let me tell now tell you a little secret, I was trained in life to be the anti bella figura guy. I'm the original anti bella figura guy. It has been ingrained in me for…well…forever.

I was trained in the art of business by the *Bing Fa*…The ancient Chinese War commentaries written twenty five hundred years ago in a book called *The Art of War* by Sung Tzu…and studied to this day by military commanders all over the world. This book has been my business "bible" my entire career.

The Art of War is a small book containing twenty-one teaching principles that are taught with short sayings and examples. The Chinese generals would study the examples and would learn from them and later would be victorious in battle. So would other military commanders over the millennia that studied this book, including every prominent American military commander there ever was.

As a lawyer, I was well versed in this book, and my copies (I had many over the years) were always dog-eared and worn out. As a matter of fact, a copy of *The Art of War* was always on my nightstand …no matter where I was.

Let me give you an example of how this philosophy…ingrained in me for decades…clashes with the concept of bella figura.

One of the teaching principles in *The Art of War* is a principle called "To catch the bear, dress like a sheep."

In ancient China, the warlords would send out hunting parties of archers in search of food for the troops. They would first find a smaller animal…maybe a sheep…kill it, skin it…and then drape the skin over an archer who would be kneeling down.

The rest of the archers would then hide in the bushes. When the bear, attracted by the scent of the blood from the sheep skin draped over the crouching archer approached the sheep all the archers would jump up from their hiding places and slay the bear thus being able to have food to feed the troops. The bear did not feel threatened as he approached the sheep and let his guard down, resulting in its death.

What this means in modern day business context is this: If, for example, you are slightly under dressed for a meeting or show up late or look harried…or (in my case) show up in an old dilapidated car… you give the indication however subtly that you are not a worthy adversary. The person that you are negotiating against will not hold you in high regard. Just the opposite, he will think that you are ill-equipped for the meeting and perhaps lower his guard. That is when you strike and usually get what you want. This is the way of the Bing Fa.

I have used this technique hundreds of times in complex negotiations over the decades, and for me it is quite effective. I would not wear a tie perhaps, or wear a sports jacket instead of a suit, something that will give a perceptive individual the idea that I am not very good competition.

In other words, I am not an empty suit as I perceive some practitioners of bella figura to be. Not all are…note I said some.

Who understands this concept in Sicily? Not many. Actually, I should not say that. Who understood the concept (but without ever learning about it from *The Art of War*), was a small subset of very successful Mafiosi that ended up dominating Sicily in the 1980s and 1990s.

While more flamboyant Mafiosi with their diamond pinkie rings and fancy cars were being assassinated by the hundreds, these men, often wearing dumpy clothing, unshaven, driving the oldest of autos, were busy wresting control of the criminal organizations away from them. While one group was practicing bella figura, the other was unknowingly practicing *The Art of War.*

Thus, Sicilians do have experience with the concept but never recognized it for what it was.

Those days, however, are long gone, and I suppose that if I want to fit in I should master this concept a bit. No, I will master it.

What I do not want to be, however, is the "Ugly American" living in Sicily and being isolated from people because of my "Americanism." Slowly I am learning to understand this big cultural difference, and I am sure that as time passes, I will have that sweater thrown on my shoulders too!

That is the plan now.

Chapter Twenty-Three

The Magic Carpet Flew Over the World Today

The Castello di Calatabiano; Alcantara, Villages of Motta Camastra, Randazzo, Cesarò, Troina, Nicosia, Leonforte, Calascibetta and Magnificent Enna

Prologue:

Vita was going to be in Sicily only two more weeks, so naturally I wanted to take one last road trip with her before she left.

She texted me one morning "I am free tomorrow…want to go on a road trip?"

As usual, the answer was one word.

"Sure," I responded.

I picked her up the next morning at 8 a.m. at Roberto's Café in Naxos. While enjoying a cup of espresso we studied the map of Sicily… actually she studied the map…and she decided our trip for the day. The only rules we always had were (1) never travel on the highways if possible…use only back roads if we can and (2) try to go to places where neither of us have been.

She chose a very ambitious plan for the day. We would head north and west up the back side of Etna and then skirt the mountain laterally in a sweeping arc and toward the late afternoon flatten out the arc and head into Enna for a quick look-see before heading home.

The terrain would be different, and difficult to drive on. Hey…I was with my sidekick Vita, so it really did not matter. We would have fun no matter what.

The route she chose would bring us literally on top of the world… in Sicily at least…as we would be traveling around Etna on a two lane road that would require a constant shifting of gears as we climbed and descended countless hills and valleys.

The Magic Carpet would indeed get a workout today. From an above sea level perspective, other than being in the crater of Etna itself, we could get no higher today. We figured that by the end of the day our road trip would cover between 250 to 300 kilometers all told through the most beautiful part of Sicily, so we wanted to get going.

We had selected five major places to stop on the way, and the first two were not far from Naxos.

"One place I was only at night, for diner" she said "and the other two I was with tour groups…but there are different things I want to see", she said.

I was in complete agreement as I had been to several of the places on her itinerary too, but traveling with Vita is always like painting on a new canvas…you never know what the picture will be until it is completed. So I agreed and off we went.

The Magic Carpet was gassed up, and in tiptop form. I had money in my pocket and an able co-pilot, so I was ready for today's adventure.

First Stop: The Castello di Calatabiano

We zipped through Naxos and several kilometers away…sitting high atop a huge mountain in on the outskirts of Caltabiano…was the Castello di Caltabiano, the ancient Greek settlement and Byzantine fortress that was later fist an Arab fortress and later a Norman fortress.

I had passed the Castello a million times over the years while traveling on the autostrada in the distance and I always wondered what it was. The fortress…on one of the highest points in the area… was visible for miles around and must have been hugely important centuries ago for strategic reasons.

We parked the car and walked up a huge hill to the entrance and straight ahead of us, climbing almost vertically up the side of the mountain, was this elevator chair lift kind of device that we had to get into in order to make it up to the castle. Spotting the visitors center, we went in to purchase the admission tickets.

A pleasant young woman greeted us and for a fourteen-euro charge, gave us the tickets and quickly showed us how to operate the lift.

Huh?

We had to operate the lift? I mean…no one will drive that thing? What happens if it breaks down, I thought to myself.

Vita read my face and gave me one of those "Don't be a baby, Alfred, I will figure it out" looks. I sheepishly got in the lift, and Vita quickly figured out how to operate the thing, and off we went.

Straight up the side of a mountain we climbed…it was awesome.

The higher we climbed the larger and more beautiful the surrounding vista became. From this vantage point, I could see the Port of Catania on my right Calabria across the horizon, and Taormina to my left… a sweeping and beautiful view. I thought to myself that someone should just charge a couple euro for giving people a ride up to the castle and back. It would be well worth it.

In any case, we soon arrived at the castle.

The castle was thousands of years old…Greek, Arab, Byzantine… truly ancient…and beautiful.

It had been completely restored in 2004 by the Sicilian government and now had a restaurant, a meeting hall and other amenities for conferences and meetings in addition to the historical component. Since it was only 9am by the time we arrived and we were the first visitors that morning, we were able to roam the castle freely and looked in every nook and cranny of the place.

This place had many stories to tell, I thought to myself.

Storage room, defense fortifications, and artifacts…you name it…were on display. Vita headed up to the highest vista point at the very top of the castle and we spent several moments taking pictures contemplating what life must have been like for the defenders.

Pretty soon, it was time to depart, and guess what happened on the way down? Yup…the lift suddenly stopped about half way down. "That's interesting," said Vita as she pushed the re-set button. The lift quickly started and within minutes we were on the ground.

Walking inside the visitor center, I said to the nice woman "Um… the lift stopped half way down, and I want to report it." Smiling at me she said, "Yes, I know. I forgot to tell you to press the re-set button if it stopped." Huh? Did she just say that to me?

In any case, I presume that they will have the lift serviced soon and I recommend that you visit this wonderful place. Here is the web site if you are interested. *http://www.castellodicalatabiano.it/index.aspx*

Stop Two: Parco Botanico e Geologico delle Gole dell'Alcantara (The Alcantara) and the quaint Village of Motta Camastra.

Movie lovers know that many scenes from the movie *The Godfather* were shot in and around locations in greater Naxos, Taormina, and its environs. Did you know that several of those scenes and several were shot in the beautiful little town of Motta Camastra?

Not far away, in a neighboring town, is the farmhouse where Michael Corleone's first wife got blown up and the train station where DeNiro arrived is not too far away. Most of the scenes that portrayed the Sicilian village of Corleone were actually filmed in and around this area. Did you know that?

While several early scenes *for The Godfather* were shot in Motta Camastra, is that what this area's claim to fame is?

Far from it.

Located at the base of Motta Camastra is *The Parco Botanico e Geologico delle Gole dell'Alcantara*. This scenic wonderland is a nature's lover's delight and with its many hiking trails, botanical gardens, gorges, and breathtaking vistas stretching over its 250 acres of pristine natural preserve. This dwarfs any movie that anyone could make.

"Alcantara" as the place is known, named for the river that flows through the gorge, is heaven on earth. Both Vita and I had been here before, but Vita wanted to show me her favorite spot, and I obliged. I always like the quiet of this place, and on this brilliant sunshine filed early morning…again with no one here…it was a truly special experience for me.

In June, July, August and September this place is teeming with tourists from all over the world, but when we went…early October, we had the place practically to ourselves.

We wandered around a bit and we looked in silence…words are inadequate to describe the park's beauty. After a while mutual glances to each other signaled it was time to move on to the town…although we really could have spent a week exploring this creation of God. The official web site is *http://www.terralcantara.it/en* if you want to take a look. This place needs at least one full day to explore…at a minimum.

The Quaint Village of Motta Camastra.

Roberto told me when we returned to Naxos later that night that a friend of his is the mayor of this special place and that if he had known we were visiting there he would have called him for us.

No matter. The place is awesome.

The village has a tiny population...only 850 people live in this heavenly place. The village is set on a gorgeous mountain top hill with narrow streets, cobble-stoned ways, and great and friendly inhabitants.

We parked the car by the "municipio"...the town offices...because I was afraid that if I parked the car anyplace else, no other cars would be able to pass. That is how narrow and picturesque the streets are!

We are both snapping pictures left and right, and quickly caught the attention of many locals...who approached us with big smiles on their faces and welcomed us to town. A local female police officer and I had a delightful conversation and Vita later and took a picture of the officer and I posing together.

What was funny was that we had to wait until the officer put her lipstick on and her official police hat... bella figura, you know! It is very important.

We stopped at an outdoor bar that had many old timers sitting outside, and for half an hour we engaged in wonderful conversation with them. Of course, someone always knows someone who lives in America and that is usually the topic of conversation.

There was something about this town and its people that appealed to me. Was it the smallness and sheer beauty of its location? Or was it the friendliness of its people? Whatever it is, I made a note that I will bring my friends here to see this place and will come back here often.

Now, it was time to leave and we both slowly walked back to the car...delaying for as long as possible our departure. What a great little place.

Stop Three: The Lovely and Spectacular Drive to Randazzo Passing Through Many Wondrous Places and Finishing with a Meal Fit for a King.

Leaving Motta, I wanted to pass through Francavilla di Sicilia, the birthplace of Gaetano Cipolla, one of my heroes in America and I wanted to see that sleepy little village that is nestled on the slopes of Etna.

Passing through town, I thought of Gaetano and how his love for this little village compelled him to greatness later in life as a professor in America. Great men, I learned, have come from many small Sicilian villages, Francavilla Di Sicilia could call Gaetano Cipolla its own.

I was happy we took this side detour.

We then turned south and passed through another lovely village town of Castigilione set high atop a beautiful vista. I made a note to come back to this area as it was covered with lush vegetation and a variety of interesting rock formations. Since we were pressed for time we headed due south and picked up Route 120, we were headed to Randazzo for lunch, as this was the place to eat according to everybody.

One thing we noticed on this stretch of the roadway was how teeming it was with life…literally…cows, sheep, horses and farm animals. We began to see scores of them…then hundreds of them… on farmland stretching as far as the eye can see.

Getting closer to Randazzo, we encountered our first two cows up close and personal…complete with cow bells...walking casually down the road! At first, I though they were bulls and rolled up my window. Then I realized that if a bull were to indeed charge the Magic Carpet, we would probably be toast in any case and relaxed a bit.

Fortunately, upon closer inspection, we found them to be just huge cows.

Vita and I were laughing at the sight as we slowly drove past the two wandering animals…until we rounded the bend and saw a bunch up the road… a whole herd…maybe twenty…of mooing cows heading right at us! I reduced the speed of the Magic Carpet to barely one mile an hour and we rolled past the herd.

It was a thrill, I will you tell you that!

This was just unbelievably beautiful and quintessentially Sicilian farmland. We had no intention of actually travelling through the town of Randazzo…rather we wanted to continue to see exactly what we were seeing…rich, beautiful, lush, colorful farmland teeming with animals on a brilliant and sunlit day.

We were listening to Dave Matthews on the iPod, and surprisingly, his music went splendidly with the atmosphere of the early afternoon ride. Bob Marley and the Whalers also worked well with the ambience of the travel for this location as well. We had both learned that the good music that accompanies the exciting visuals we were experiencing really has enhanced all our road trips, and my trusty iPod…with almost 2000 songs load in it…has proven up to task.

All this driving and sightseeing now had made us famished, so we needed to stop and ask someone where a decent trattoria was located. We wanted to sample the local cuisine very thoroughly!

Heavenly Lunch

I briefly pulled the car over in the Randazzo vicinity while Vita ran into a roadside bar to get refreshed. As I was waiting for her, a truck with four men pulled up along side and looked at me. "Uh, oh," I thought to myself. The men were big and burly. As it turns out, they were really nice guys.

The guy on the passenger side asked me if I was from the area, and I told him where I was from. Broad smiles broke out on all four men as they each had cousins living in Brooklyn and in Paramus, New Jersey. In any case, they suggested a trattoria about four kilometers down the road, and since we were in meat country…they all suggested the lamb, the sausage or the pork. "You will never forget the meal," my newly found friend Alfredo (from Giarre) told me. "Come, follow me…we are passing right by."

When Vita got in the car, she had a quizzical look on her face. "Not to worry" I said, "they know a good place to eat".

Did I say a good place to eat? No…I mean a great place to eat. No, I mean a heavenly and wondrous place to eat. If you eat meat, that is. You see, in the middle of the back end of Etna, you do not order fish. As a matter of fact, not a single fish item was on the menu.

Only two things were on the menu: Home made pasta…many kinds…and meat…sausages, lamb, pork…made in a variety of ways… far too confusing for us to be honest.

Even though I watch ever morsel of meat that I eat (maybe one time a month), if I was going to go, this was an appropriate place to go down swinging, I thought to myself. I asked the lovely hostess if she could prepare two plates of meat for us…a little of everything to sample. She said of course she could do that.

Vita wanted to sample the local cheeses too, so that was it…meat, cheese, salad with tomatoes, bread, extra virgin olive oil …along with a half liter of local red wine . What else could you ask for?

I ask you, what can possibly be better than this meal for a guy?

It was a carnivore's delight.

Well, the ambience of this wonderful rustic trattoria rivaled the food. This was a rustic farmhouse restaurant…right out of a storybook. We sat by a window and watched the sheep, cows and horses graze in the lush meadow. They were probably tomorrow's special offerings at the trattoria, but they certainly made a special picture during lunch, that's for sure!

Here it was…a lovely Tuesday October afternoon, and Vita and I feasting…and I mean feasting…on delicious (but for me, forbidden) meat. The bread was just unbelievable, the olive oil was a familiar brand that Roberto's serves at his place, so I knew it was good. Vita really loved the cheeses. The wine was hearty, robust, it had great bouquet and tasted wonderful…and the meat…all I can say is three words "oh my God."

Vita would later complain for the next few hours about eating "too much fat" as we gallivanted over hill and dale, but for this moment frozen in time, we both were in culinary heaven.

What was the bill for this feast? By feast I mean two huge plates overflowing with roasted meats of all kinds…31 euro…about $36USD. Honestly, in the states, the wine alone would have cost this amount. This was a $150 meal in Boston…and Boston would not be able to compete even for one second with this place.

Where were we you ask? I happened to take a card. If you ever in Sicily, and want to eat the best meat in Sicily, go to this place: *Don Santo Trattoria…*Strada Statale no. 11, Randazzo-Capo d' Orlando at Km 15-Favoscuro. Here is the web site: *www.donsanto.it*

After an hour of feasting, we rolled to the car. We had territory to cover and we had to get to Enna, which was still 130 kilometers away.

Stop Four: The Hundred Times We Stopped as We Rode Harder Than the Lone Ranger.

The afternoon itinerary was simple.

We planned to follow Route 120 from Randazzo and meander all the way to Enna. Route 120 is a flattened way, completely circumventing any highway. We planned on traveling through the magical agricultural towns of Cesarò, Troina, Nicosia, and then heading south in a corkscrew manner into Leonforte, Calascibetta before reaching Enna.

Heading out from Randazzo for about thirty kilometers, I must have shifted gears a thousand times. The Magic Carpet was really straining as we climbed one mountainous road, drove around yet another hair-pin turn, and dodged flocks of sheep, goats and cows. This was farm country, primarily country for raising animals, and the vistas that opened up before us as we rounded each curve or valley differed for what we had seen only one kilometer behind us.

Things in this section of the roadway were full of fall colors and vegetation...scenic farms dotted the countryside, and when we hit each of the towns as we progressed on our journey, we understood the strategic and visual importance of each. Each of these little villages and cities essentially supplied the farmers of the areas for perhaps a twenty to thirty kilometer radius. These towns offered central marketplaces, transport for their products, supplies, and over the years, diverse cultural activities and festas for the people.

I had a couple of observations on this stretch of terrain, which really was the longest portion of the drive. A visitor cannot drive route 120 at night. Between the rough conditions of the road...I was forever dodging this hole or that one...and the fact that absolutely no streetlights are on this mountainous road, our decision to travel at this time of the day a prudent one. I would not try to drive this road at nighttime.

Another observation: About thirty kilometers west of Randazzo... just past Cesaro... the landscape completely changed. This was mega-agricultural country now...no horses, sheep or cows, no quaint farmhouses. It looked to us that these enormous farms were probably owned by huge conglomerates and with the harvest already in, a moon-like landscape effect took over as we travelled through many kilometers of land devoid of crops and vegetation.

The land, as a matter of fact, had been tilled and turned in preparation for the planting of the next crop. At one high point in this section of the trip, we crossed a huge windmill farm, passing through scores of enormous windmills that generated power for the area.

It was eerie to see this, to be honest.

Many times we stopped the car and Vita hopped out to take a photo here and there. We accumulated over 200 images on this trip, and this section of Sicily was certainly much different that the section that we started out in the morning.

When we hit Nicosia, we decided to break for an espresso and to refresh ourselves a bit. Driving through this lively town, its main street was quite narrow. Many many people were sitting on both sides of the streets just engaging in late afternoon conversation and looking at the passing cars. Strangely, almost everybody was a man. Vita said to me that no self-respecting woman would sit on the sidewalk in a chair and gawk at passers by. I agreed with her.

On the outskirts of town we found an espresso bar and stopped the car to rest a bit and refresh ourselves. This part of the drive had been tough on me driving wise, but I was glad to have seen this stretch of Sicily.

While Vita was refreshing herself, I struck up a conversation with some nice men who directed me to the nearest gas station and also to route 111...which ultimately would lead us to Enna. The other thing that I watch when I travel the back roads of Sicily is to never let the gas tank get below a half tank. In the mountains of Etna, especially unfamiliar terrain, a breakdown or running out of gas would be disastrous. My New England "A penny of prevention prevents a pound of cure" motto really helps me on these trips.

Vita is the trip director, and I am the security director...a perfect combination!

Stop Five: The Magical and Beautiful Town of Enna

It was becoming late in the day, and I wanted to get to Enna before dusk as Vita had never been there and I wanted to show her the main sights.

That meant two things: (a) We had to cover the last 68 kilometers relatively quickly and (b) we would only be able to see some of the major sights in Enna.

Driving down route 117 from Nicosia to Leonforte and from Leonforte to Enna was no easy task. The sun was at that point where it was hitting us full on in the windshield and I had a time negotiating the terrain and keeping on the road because of sun glare. At one point, within a half-mile stretch, there were three hairpin turns...and

I noticed that the railings on the roadway were not so sturdy. Still, we made the best of it, and by the time we hit Enna, the sun was setting and dusk was upon us.

I had been to Enna many times. As a matter of fact, I have witnessed the profoundly beautiful Good Friday processions there three different times and even wrote about it in one of my previous books. I adore Enna.

Enna, located almost exactly in the center of Sicily, was at one time was an enormously important strategic town. Sitting high atop a mountain, whoever controlled Enna controlled the surrounding area.

The Greeks, Romans, Arabs, Normans and most recently the Spanish all realized this, and the most recent occupiers…the Spanish…left an indelible mark on this town. It is really a beautiful town and should be visited by you when you come to Sicily.

Pulling into town, we fought the "going back to work after siesta" rush hour traffic (bumper to bumper…straight uphill…and me driving a stick shift car…geez). When we pulled onto Via Roma…the main tourist street and main attraction area, low and behold we found one of the greatest parking spots in the history of the world!

Right in front of the Hotel Sicilia…about half way up Via Roma… was a nifty little parking spot waiting for us!

It was chilly when we got out of the car…the winds of the evening were cold…and both of us added a layer of clothing as we walked about.

Enna at night is lovely. People were milling around, shops, bars, and restaurants. The town was abuzz with activity. Even though it was a bit chilly, it was perfect walking around weather.

Our first stop, of course, was the *Duomo* on Via Roma…that Baroque centerpiece of the Good Friday procession. While the outside of the *Duomo* is nothing spectacular, the inside certainly is, with its high arching ceiling, and beautiful altar. Vita simply could not take her eyes off the ceiling. It is magnificent, as is the entire *Duomo*. It really is a great place to see.

We then walked to the end of Via Roma to see the centerpiece of the whole area, the strategically important (during ancient times at least) *Castello dei Lombardi* or the Lombard Castle, built in the thirteenth century by Frederick. Unfortunately, the castle had just closed for the day and we were not able to take a tour, but the ambiance of the surrounding and superbly lit facade made this quite a romantic and picturesque setting.

We lingered on the railing for a while, looking at the villages below, all aglow with the evening lights. It was an unforgettable scene.

We then walked slowly down the Via Roma, enjoying the evening, enjoying the sights and sounds of such a foreign yet friendly place, and by the time we had walked the end of the Via Roma, we decided to find a place for a …beer! Yes, we both were in the mood for a beer, and we found the perfect place.

By this time of the early evening, we had been on the road for thirteen hours and had covered some hard terrain. Not wanting a huge meal, a beer and an arancini each did the trick. However, it was the companionship and small talk that made the moment memorable.

We had spent a lot of time this summer traveling the length of Sicily together, and a firm and fast, and I am sure, everlasting friendship had formed. This road trip was coming to an end, and I was happy that I was able to see the sights of today with my favorite travel companion.

The ride back to Naxos was cerebral. We engaged in somewhat emotional conversation. I mentioned to her that I was sad that this was our last road trip together.

She looked at me and said "Maybe not. Maybe next week we can do another if I can find the time."

As usual, I gave my same answer "Sure…just tell me when."

Pulling into Naxos ninety minutes later, we were both exhausted but content. Who wouldn't be? We had just been to the top of the world with the Magic Carpet and there was a chance that we could do it again next week!

Chapter Twenty-Four

More Places

1. Catania: Ognina and Via Crociferi

A. Ognina

I have been to Catania a million times and probably have complained about the lack of parking and the dirt on some of the side streets a million and one times.

However, the nightlife there is terrific and the restaurants are just great. Like any metropolitan city, different districts have their own ambiance. In the past I have written about the central district and also the port district and also the touristic district and now I want to tell you about two contrasting areas that I really enjoy: the fishing area of Ognina and the stately baroque street of Via Crociferi.

Ognina is actually closer to my house in Aci Catena than it is to the downtown district in Catania. It is on the *lungomare*, a beautiful stretch of shoreline that runs from Catania to Aci Castello. Ognina is located in the northeast part of the city, heading out of town. The harbor of Ognina is very beautiful and small boats and pleasure craft clog the marina named Ulysses all summer long.

I also love this area because of the many take-out fish shacks and food kiosks where, for a few euro, you can have an excellent lunch. My favorite disco is right there on the water as well....Luna 69... which does not open until 11pm on the weekends and doesn't close until 4am. Many a night I have enjoyed observing the young crowd there and the pulsating disco music while nursing my ten-euro beer!

In the fall, street vendors hawk the most delicious roasted chestnuts you will ever eat, too. I make a special trip there on Sundays in October just to buy a bag! They are big, moist...and just heavenly to eat!

Ognina was always a workingman's district, like South Boston is back in the states. Blue collar workers and fishermen lived exclusively in the area at one time, but over the past few years high rise apartments have sprung up by the water and the Catanese version of yuppies now occupy stretches of the area.

It is slowly becoming the waterfront suburbia of Catania.

While many people flock to the shore here for water activities like swimming, the lava rocks make it uncomfortable for me to navigate the shoreline, and I always go to other areas nearby to swim. However, the ambiance of the area is great and I love to visit the *Shrine of Our Lady of Ognina* too…located close to the water on the street.

The *Feast of Santa Maria di Ognina* is an annual celebration held every September. It is a week long celebration featuring street vendors, fireworks, processions and of course, plenty of food. Last year I observed the statue of the Virgin Mary as it was paraded through the area streets and was impressed by the fervor of the faithful.

The firework display always was terrific too!

A dear friend from my hometown, Nunzio DiMarca was born here before he moved to the states, and tears swell in his eyes when we talk of the area. His daughter Tina Fosman tries to make it back to Sicily as often as possible to visit her uncle Carman who returned to Sicily. The entire family longs for the day when they can all be here together. Ognina is truly a special place for many and you should spend some time here too.

B. Catania-Via Crociferi

Via Crociferi, set in Catania's central district and stretching way out of town, presents to visitors perhaps the finest example of Baroque architecture in all of Sicily.

My adopted daughter Catia Barra…an experienced tour guide and a perfect example of the modern Sicilian woman...took me one Sunday afternoon ten years ago to walk the streets of this magnificent area of Catania for the first time and taught me to appreciate the true art of these buildings.

Via Crociferi is named after the Crociferi fathers and their magnificent church, *St. Camillo.*

At the end of the seventeenth century,1693 to be exact, a devastating earthquake centered near Noto and Calabria with violent aftershocks almost completely destroyed Catania and this was followed by violent tsunamis that wiped out a large portion of the population. The city was slowly re-built in Baroque style afterwards and by the eighteenth century this area became the cornerstone area for the monastic orders that lived in Catania.

Within about 300 yards or so of each other are four churches. *St. Benedetto, St. Francesco Borgia, St. Giuliano* and *St. Camillo*, which form the centerpiece of the area…each filled with stunning examples of the dark lava stone architecture and these forms run up and into the *Villa Cerami*, which now houses the University of Catania Law School.

I will never forget the Benedictine nuns who are housed in the convent nearby and the beautiful hymns that they sing. One year I watched them sing the Ave Maria during the *Feast of Saint Agatha*. Chills went up my spine that evening, as I listened to these angels on earth sing.

Baroque architecture, by the way runs all the way to Acireale, so if you are an aficionado of beauty, then this is a good day adventure for you. As I wrote a few chapters ago, Ragusa Ibla and Modica have great Baroque architecture too.

A quick note on the earthquake of 1693 in Catania:

On January 11, 1693 a devastating earthquake struck Sicily, Malta and Calabria and is still considered the most powerful earthquake in Italian history. According to the research that I did online, over seventy towns were destroyed and causing the death of about 60,000 people . Baroque architecture rose from the ashes of the destruction of Catania and stands today as a testament to the violence that befell Catania.

According to the online research that I did, a wide swath of eastern Sicily was destroyed, with the epicenter being around Noto. I saw evidence of the destruction firsthand when I visited Ragusa, Messina, Catania, Modica, Noto, and many other smaller villages as I travelled about. Remnants of this devastating earthquake over three hundred and twenty years ago still scar the terrain as well. However, the resilient Sicilians re-built many areas and the Baroque architecture of many towns now stands as testament to the destruction that occurred.

How bad was the destruction? About 63% of Catania's population was killed (over 12,000 people) and over 5,000 of Ragusa's population (over 50%) were killed as well. Somewhere between 50,000 to 60,000 were killed all told. It was a terrible catastrophe that forever changed the landscape of Sicily.

2. San Giovanni La Punta, Viagrande, Zafferana Dell'Etna, Trecastagni, Pedara, Nicolosi, and Sant'Alfio… "The Paese Etna"

These small villages that surround the south and east sides of Etna are some of my favorite places to go in the whole Etna region. In the previous chapter I wrote about Randazzo and points north and west. This are is east of those places, heading toward the water. If you look at a map of the Etna area, stringing these villages together on a half-day is the best way to get the flavor of the area.

San Giovanni La Punta

You can approach the first stop, San Giovanni La Punta, via the autostrada, or by the shore road from Catania, Route 114. Sooner or later, you be able to pick up a road sign for San Giovanni La Punta.

This village actually has a huge shopping center on the outskirts called Le Zagra that is filled with all sorts of shops and stores. This is a mid-priced shopping area, and will not break the bank. Need something to take home with you? This is the place. San Giovanni La Punta's main street is nothing special to write home about, a typical Catania suburb, but the pastries and wine here are splendid.

On the way out (find the road sign indications to Viagrande…the signs are good in this area), stop by the Hotel Paradiso Dell'Etna and see the place that was once the Nazi headquarters in the area during the Second World War. This beautiful hotel was confiscated by the Germans and was used by Rommel when he was here. I have dined at the restaurant and it is truly a great experience. This is a great little town full of lovely little churches and sanctuaries too.

Viagrande

Viagrande is a small town adjacent to San Giovanni La Punta and features my favorite bar/pizzeria, Café Urna, and also my favorite restaurant in the area, Piccolo Mundo. Café Urna was used as a German hospital and then as a British field hospital during the Second World War. But, for many decades it has been a favorite gelateria and pizzeria owned by the Giuffreda family. The granita during the summer is special, as well as their gelato. When you see their pastry selection, you will faint!

One time, I bumped into English people who were staying at the Hotel Paradiso Dell' Etna in San Giovanni La Punta and they asked me to suggest a good restaurant to them, and I suggested Piccolo Mondo. They ended going back there four times for dinner! If you do go there to eat, try the roasted meats or the roasted fish plates…heavenly. Tell Carmelo the owner, who will entertain you with his singing, that I send my regards! The center of town is picturesque and the park is a wonderful place for a nice walk after dinner.

Zafferana Dell'Etna

Zafferana Dell' Etna…straight up road from Viagrande is a great place to eat sausage, buy local honey, or sample their heavenly locally made liqueurs or their wine. Every October they have the Oktoberfest on Sundays and it is a treat walking around town sampling things. During the week, visit the Duomo too. You will be pleasantly surprised.

Recently my friend Steve Carbone and I spent a few hours in town and we had lunch at a local restaurant. Pasta, sausage, fresh bread, bottled water; liter of red wine…the bill was thirteen euro! It was great!

You will love this great village…I do!

Trecastagni

From Zafferana Dell'Etna, find the road signs and head to my ancestral village of Trecastagni. Here you need to see three places: first, you need to see the *Church of Saint Alfio* in the Sant'Alfio Plaza and home of the 1300 hundred year old festival, the Festa di Sant' Alfio, which is held on May 9-10 every year and attended by tens of thousands of faithful. Afterwards, head to the Piazza Marconi, where the municipal office are located, and enjoy a walk around the piazza among the palm trees and fountain and then stop and have an espresso at the bar on the corner.

From there you can follow the road sign to the *Matrice or* Mother Church, set high on the best observation spot in the area. From this location, you will be able to see a spectacular vista of the lowlands below, which stretches from the port of Catania on one side to Taormina on the other. This is truly a remarkable sight! Obviously, I am prejudiced about this wonderful town…it has such special meaning to me…but I promise you that you will enjoy it a lot!

Pedara

As you leave Trecastagni, you will find the road sign to Pedara, the small sister town of Trecastagni known for its fabled wine and bread shops. This cobblestoned village has an ancient section that is also very nice to wander about and several great restaurants and pizzerias. The light color stonework is an interesting juxtaposition between the lava rock used and the light sandstone work of the churches and buildings. During the day, many shops that dot the roadway are open selling all sorts of artesian things. It is a bargain-hunters delight!

Nicolosi

From Pedara, you can follow the indications to Nicolosi…the highest point on this side of Etna and which borders the Etna Park itself. Here the air is crisp, clean and a little chilly in the late season.

You will see stands of trees very tall and elegant housing all around. Many wealthy northern Italians own summer homes here and the town is immaculate. Find the old section of Nicolosi and park your car and wander about. It is a lovely experience. Nicolosi and Pedara, by the way, have some of Sicily's best health clinics and spas.

Sant' Alfio

From Nicolosi, you want to travel laterally now to Sant' Alfio… the road is clearly marked…and stop in this quaint town to see the *Church of Sant Alfio*, and the fantastic panoramic view of the entire area. You must sample the pistachio and almond cookies at the bar in the square right by the church. You will be in heaven when you do!

This abbreviated trip, which should take you a half day to six hours to accomplish, is a wonderful way to spend time and get to know the area.

One cautionary note: Since you are travelling on mountain roads, plan your day accordingly. If you arrive in San Giovanni La Punta relatively early in the morning, then by mid-afternoon you should be headed back down the mountain. It is better to travel here during the daylight than at nighttime.

That bit of advice aside, you will love this adventure!

Chapter Twenty-Five

42 Orchard Street and Zina

This heroic lady has passed on years ago, but I want to pay her homage today.

You know her. Her name may be different, but you know her. Every Sicilian immigrant family had a Zina, and she was mine.

She was my grandmother. She was my dad's mother… a small peanut-sized hero who passed on at the age of ninety-eight years old many years ago. It must have been tough for her to live so long because she died a few years after burying her son, my dad.

However, I never heard this woman complain about anything.

Of the many regrets that I have in my life, right up there near the top of the list is the fact that I never thanked her enough for the life-long sacrifices that she made. First for the sacrifices on behalf of her son, and then for her grandkids (me, my brother, my sister)…and finally for a while there, for her great grandkids.

I want to say it now, I want to say it publicly, and I want the world to know: Thank you, nana.

Beside the obvious physical things…the endless clothes, toys, money and things that she was always giving us…or the portion of our high school and college education that contributed too...that stuff is obvious. I want to thank her for the intangibles.

I want to thank her example that she set for all of us. She, like hundreds of thousands of other Sicilian immigrants who came here and slaved in the hopes for a better day for their families, set the example that I try to follow to this day.

Her story is a familiar one; she came here from Sicily barely a teenager along with her sisters and brothers. She was in the middle age-wise with her siblings, and at least two of her siblings were very small children when they arrived here on the banana boat.

The only difference was that she and her siblings were orphans.

Her parents had died in the influenza scourge that affected Sicily in the early twentieth century and are buried someplace in Sicily. One of my projects on my to-do list here in Sicily is to hunt their burial plot down, and this year I learned information as to a possible location.

Next year, when I return, I will find the Lascola grave, I hope.

What I do know is that her dad worked for the railroad, and that the family often travelled with him. As a matter of fact, my grandmother would tell me that her brothers and sisters were born in different parts of Sicily, along the same railway route.

I say that she told me things but that is not exactly the complete picture. You see, Zina was in the states over seventy years and never learned English. She spoke Sicilian, which I heard in my house my whole life. Hers was a form of ancient Sicilian spoken in Sicily almost a hundred years ago.

As a matter of fact, I recall on my first trip here many years ago speaking this dialect not knowing that words, pronunciation, inflection and Italian had crept into life in Sicily. When I spoke this dialect, people would smile and say to me laughing "I haven't heard those words since I was small…how quaint."

Zina and her sisters and cousins worked in the sweatshops of Lawrence Massachusetts, along with thousands of other Sicilian immigrants.

In those days, the garment industry was huge in Massachusetts along the Merrimack Valley corridor, and garment manufacturers and shoe shops were the major source of employment.

For you historians out there, the Bread and Roses Strike in 1912 was when Italian immigrants finally had had enough of workplace abuse and protested against greedy mill owners and demonstrated for weeks, ending in violence and death for some. It had a huge impact on American law which led to big changes in the child labor laws in America and happened right around the corner where Zina would work a few years later.

Like all the young immigrant girls and women who worked in the sweatshops, they worked piecemeal, in other words, they got paid only for what they did. So the work was long, and hard, and for not much money.

Cousins had sponsored Zina and her sibling's immigration to America. They lived in the family apartment building at 42 Orchard Street, Lawrence Massachusetts, where she lived almost her entire life.

This apartment building was my home away from home. My

house was located only about 400 yards, just three blocks down. In those days, the immigrants were all living in a ten-block radius from what is considered its mecca, Common Street, where the first group of arriving immigrants lived. Orchard Street was two blocks up from Common Street.

The first floor of 42 Orchard Street had a bakery, and right across the street was the chicken store where patrons would pick out a live chicken, watch as the chicken's necks were stretched, and then placed in boiling water to pluck the feathers, and that was it…supper that evening.

My friend's grandfather owned this chicken store and he is now a prominent area doctor. It is funny how people have such humble beginnings, isn't it?

The apartment building had six apartments on the upper floors, all inhabited by my relatives. Every Friday night, my dad (who was born and brought up in this very same apartment) brought my brother and myself over and we would stay the night, sometimes two, with Zina and my grandfather Alfio.

The apartment was great…at least for a little kid.

First, my brother and I slept on a green fold out couch that was cool because this room was the television room and featured a small black and white television. In those days, no one knew about snowy reception, digital television, and guess what? We had a choice of two… and then three stations to choose from! Wow! Three stations!

Zina would always spoil us all weekend too. There was always our favorite food to eat…plus cupcakes or "push-ups"…that ice cream in a cardboard that you "pushed up" and ate. In those days, people gave little thought to sugar content, treats or the like. It was an era that is long gone and the innocence of that era had not yet influenced dietary things…especially sweets.

Later at night, we would watch her do the laundry. She had this laundry machine that had a hand operated roller that you put the clothes through a wringer as it was called, and I always used to love when she let us do that! There was this little hose attached to the washing machine (which had wheels…it rolled!) that she would put into the bathtub to empty the washing machine after the wash was done. We loved putting our hands in the water and watching Zina going crazy when she caught us. This meant an immediate bath after she scrubbed the tub!

After our Friday night bath, we were allowed to watch a little television before she would rock us to sleep, singing a church hymn. As I type these words, as a matter of fact, I can hear her sing in my head the words to the chapel song "Oh Virgin Mary…Mother of good counsel…"

I do not know if you recall that church hymn, but I rocked to sleep the first seven years of my life, every Friday night, to that hymn.

As I got older, we were allowed to watch the Friday Night Fights sponsored by Gillette and we became life long boxing fans as a result. My brother Tom, and his wife Ellen actually wrote a great boxing book later in life, and I often wonder of he remembers these nights spent watching the greats from the 1950s engage in some of the greatest bouts ever.

Saturday mornings meant cartoons on the television and that was always a treat too. Sometimes, they were not cartoons per se but weekly serials television shows: "Captain Midnight", "Sky King, "Rin Tin Tin" and of course "The Cisco Kid" and "The Roy Rogers Show" were staples of Saturday mornings! Gosh, do I miss those days!

Later in the day, we had to help Zina scrub the wooden steps of the three floors of the apartment! Each tenant took a turn every six weeks scrubbing the steps and when it was their turn, the steps had to be first swept and then scrubbed with a hand brush. These steps to this apartment building were so clean that there was never a speck of dirt on them…ever.

I remember that we had a toy drawer where all our toys were stored. We could only play in the kitchen, never in the formal living room because the furniture (which always had the clear plastic store bought covering on it) was where the "new" furniture was. The furniture remained "new" for thirty years!

It made no matter to us; the doors to every apartment were always left open and we were free to roam…and to eat…where we wanted. Zina's sister lived across the hall, my grandfather's sister downstairs, and cousins had the other three places. Gosh, what good memories!

Christmas was really memorable at 42 Orchard Street. In those days, no one had big trees. They all had smaller ones because the apartments were small. What they did have, however, was these Christmas lights that were filled with fluid that when heated made these little bubbles. We just loved watching the lights and the bubbles percolate all night long. Every apartment also had candles in the windows too. I can still feel the warmth and love of those days today...I really can… and I miss it.

During the week, Zina's day would start off with her attending the 6 a.m. Mass for immigrants in the downstairs chapel at the Holy Rosary Church. She would attend Mass every day; she did this all her life. At night, when she was older, she said the rosary. Come to think of it, she was a holy woman. She was a very holy woman.

After mass, she would work all day in the sweatshop, come home and prepare dinner for her husband, and then the both of them would walk to my house where she would help my mom by doing the ironing, etc. She did this without ever complaining or saying a word. In those days, this is what was done.

This went on for decades.

As they older, my dad finally moved them away from 42 Orchard Street to an apartment next door to us at 105 Haverhill Street in Lawrence. This was great for us because this apartment was literally next-door, and we went there often...every day, as a matter of fact… to see them, to have dinner, or to visit.

One of the most poignant visuals that I have was walking into their apartment one day when they were very old (I was twenty four or twenty five years old, I think) and seeing my father shaving his now elderly dad, my grandfather. That scene still chokes me up when I think about it. It was then that I began to think that the people that I loved would not be around forever.

In a sense, my dad, toward the end of life for his father, became his father's father! Later in life, the scene would be repeated except me, my brother and my sister would assume the role of caretakers for our parents. What comes around goes around, right?

When my grandfather passed away in the mid-seventies (right

before the birth of my daughter Jennifer, fulfilling the saying "One dies, another is born," Zina moved in with mom and dad, and stayed with them for years.

She would see her son die years later too, and after that she lived with mom for a couple of years. At some point we stepped in and put her in assisted living where we would visits her every day.

She died a dignified death at age 98, living a life of example for my family and me.

Why am I writing this story now…years after she passed?

Simple.

As I was packing my things in America in preparation for my move here to Sicily, I found Zina's prayer book that she used every day when attending Mass at Holy Rosary. It is small book, maybe five inches long and four inches wide. It would always be in her pocketbook. It was filled with religious pictures too…those pictures when people died and they have a saint's picture on one side and a prayer on another. Some of them were absolutely beautiful.

As I was leafing through the book in America, I found something that moved me; when I went to Sicily for the first time back in the 1990s, I had given Zina my ticket stub because she had asked for it. Here, among her most treasured possessions, I found that ticket stub that I had given to her years before,

Now, this prayer book is on my night stand beside my bed in Sicily. I brought it with me. I brought Zina back to Sicily with me and every night I read it for a few minutes. I read the Hail Mary and The Our Father and the Apostles' Creed...in Italian.

Yes, I struggle with the Italian but it comforts me to know that the very words that I am reading are the very words that she read every day for decades.

I think she would like that. She was fiercely Sicilian, and I think that she would be happy knowing that her grandson brought with him to Sicily her most prized possession.

I love you, Zina…and thank you for everything. I really meant that too.

Chapter Twenty-Six

The Last Road Trip- Saving the Best for Last: Lentini, Buccheri, Portopalo, Pachino, Marzamemi, Noto

Prelude:

The day was fast approaching that I was dreading. Vita was departing in five days and I was not too happy about it.

Traveling all over Sicily these past five months with her had been a real journey of discovery for me and quite an eye opener in terms of really seeing Sicily and her beauty. Along the way, I had found a new best friend and now she was leaving. The sun would not shine as brightly nor would the colors of the Sicilian countryside be as brilliant without her at my side experiencing whatever it was we were doing and wherever it was we were seeing. Whatever it did that she did to me creativity-wise was coming to an end soon and I was a little down about it.

On Monday morning, which was five days before her departure date, I received a text message from her: "Am free tomorrow. I can go on road trip if you want. You pick where we go."

Digging out the map and spreading it out on kitchen table to select one final trip with her, I happily texted her back: "Sure."

That pretty much meant that at 8 a.m. the following morning, I would meet her at Roberto's Café and off we would go.

I knew where I wanted to go: south.

I wanted to make a stop first in the wonderful little hill town of Buccheri in order to show her the wonderful sights, to buy some olive oil for myself and for her to experience the breathtaking beauty of this special town. Then I wanted to head further south to Portopalo and treat her to lunch at my favorite fish restaurant in Sicily. And, after lunch, show her the areas around Pachino and the beach resort town of Marzamemi.

It wasn't until later in the day...I think because we didn't want the day to end actually, that we added Noto to the itinerary. If you are going to see Noto, nighttime is the best time, so that was the late addition to the itinerary. Noto and the ride home will be the subject of the next chapter because today would be a jam-packed day and I want to experience it again as I write these words.

The Magic Carpet was all gassed up, my wallet had a few extra euro in it, the sun was shining as I headed to Naxos the next morning to get Vita. I knew that the line-up of places that we were going to visit would make this a very special day.

Part One: Off We Go to Lentini

Maria Grazia opens Café Sikelia every morning and I think she likes the quiet time. I know this: I love Maria Grazia and I treasure my time with her too. When I arrived at the Café at quarter to eight, I found her in the kitchen making the day's supply of fresh cornetti for the customers who would begin to arrive shortly for their espresso, cappuccino, granita, or whatever it was they have for breakfast.

When I usually arrive to the Café, I come a little early also to chat with Maria Grazia, help her if she needs help and to spend some time with a very special woman, friend and little sister. Over the years we had become like brother and sister, and to spend time in the early morning quiet before the day starts was a special time for me. She lives in Holland six months a year with her fiancée and comes home to help the family during the busy summer months. I always said that Maria Grazia was a true daughter of Sicily: strong, independent, intelligent, profoundly beautiful, and a tireless worker too.

After greeting me with the customary kiss on both cheeks and a hug, she made me an espresso and I told her our plans for the day.

Vita was popular in Sikelia with Maria Grazia, her sister Sonja, her brother Roberto and everyone else too. All summer, Vita had held her organizational meeting with her visiting Lithuanian and Russian tourists at the Café, and a deep friendship had developed between them all. It was great to see the mutual admiration society that had formed between everyone.

Working so much in the Café as well as running a boutique with her other sister Nancy, Maria Grazia would often ask me where we were going and I would fill her in on our activities. Sometimes when I would return from this road trip or that road trip with Vita she would still be at the Café, and the first thing she would do is ask us if we enjoyed ourselves, and usually I would describe to her first the day's adventure.

Thus, it was always like she was in the back seat with us...as was Roberto and Sonja too...since everyone loved the both of us. When I told her where we had planned to go that day, she mentioned that we would have a great time and told us, as always, "Be careful, OK?" Smiling at her, I would always say: "Certo!"...Certainly!

In a matter of minutes, Vita arrived, and Maria-Grazia would make Vita a "latte macchiato" ...which was a double espresso in a glass cup topped with hot frothy milk. This was Vita's morning drink of choice, along with a banana for breakfast.

It is funny how I was getting to know her foibles, I thought to myself.

Since we had to get to Lentini to take a photograph of a special place and wanted to start the day's adventure from that point which was about forty miles away from Naxos, we headed to the autostrada to pick up some time.

Luckily, as always when we start our day early, we were ahead of the morning Catanese rush hour traffic and flew through the tollbooth in Acireale in short order. We picked up the Tangenziale...the highway that circumnavigates Catania and continued in a wide arc around Catania...actually continuing to head south as it by-passes Catania

The sea was on our left and the sun was just breaking through on this glorious morning. Right after the exit for Fontanarossa Airport, Catania's busy international airport, we picked up the indications for Siracusa because the road to Lentini was to be found heading to Siracusa.

In twenty minutes we arrived at Lentini.

This stop was kind of an appetizer stop. By that I mean that we had no plans to park the car and wander about. Rather, I wanted to find the Church of Sant' Alfio and photograph it. Lentini was the place that my patron saints from Trecastagni, Saints Alfio, Filadelfo and Cirino, three teenagers who were martyred by the Romans for refusing to give up their Christian faith, were imprisoned. They were later put to death for their beliefs.

Lentini, along with Trecastagni, and the small Etna Village of Sant' Alfio celebrate an annual Festa di Sant'Alfio" every May 9th and 10th. Since I had been to the other two churches, I wanted to complete the picture in my mind and photograph this one too.

For twenty minutes we took an auto tour of Lentini…nothing spectacular except the older section. It seemed like most towns in this area have an older section and a newer section to them, and the newer section is like many other Sicilian towns. However, the older section has a lovely set of closely built neighborhoods of a baroque nature that we enjoyed looking at and then in the plaza in the heart of the old section we found the church.

As is the case with the other two Sant'Alfio churches, I was emotionally happy to see this one and Vita jumped out of the car and took several shots for me. Our rudimentary mission was complete here and we soon left town to find Buccheri. I will return here next May 10th as I want to see the festival from this town's perspective, I thought to myself as we left. Nice little town overall we both agreed, and a pleasant one too.

Part Two: Magical Buccheri

I call it "Magical Buccheri." Vita was far more succinct. She said simply "I love this place and I want to live here."

From a woman who has been all over the world and has lived in the most exotic places imaginable, I took that simple statement as an indication that she liked this place. Here is the story:

The road from Lentini to Buccheri, route 259, is a small lazy road that wanders through the lush Sicilian farmland of this part of the country, west of Siracusa. As opposed to what we saw on the back end of Etna last week when we saw viewed huge agricultural farms and the huge fields used for vegetable growing, here it is all about essentially three things: citrus (lemon and orange trees), grapes (both for eating and for wine production), and olive trees (in my opinion, the best olive oil in all of Sicily is in this region.)

As a result, the color green, in every imaginable shade, enveloped us, awed, us, and thrilled us. Simply put, the ride to Buccheri… especially starting from route 259 where you see the first road sign indications for Buccheri… got increasingly fantastic the higher up the elevation that we travelled.

Buccheri sits atop the Iblei Mountain, and is an old town. Its most recent occupiers, the Spanish, loved this place and it is well preserved and breathtaking both on its approach and also in the town itself. The ancient Romans thought so highly of the olives from this place that they were sometimes used as trading currency. With its smooth, fruit and peppery finish, tasting this olive oil is an unforgettable experience.

I had been here many times, as years ago I imported thousands of liters of oil from this area that drove my customers in America wild. It was a sad day indeed when I was notified that the four business partners in Buccheri that I was doing business with had closed down their company because of personality disputes.

Today, I wanted to buy two liters of this magic oil; one liter for myself, and one liter for Vita's father in Lithuania, who I knew would appreciate its complex composition.

I had told Vita the story of Buccheri as we drove along the road to the town. Actually, on this day we talked about many things and did many things that we had not done on other trips.

On all previous trips, the scenery that did the talking, augmented by selections of music that visually gave to the both of us a never-ending string of one spectacular visual after another.

We had now traveled the length and breadth of Sicily…on both coasts and its heartland, and our silence as we observed the passing scenery is what I remember most, as if two special friends were watching a special movie together. I think we both thought that there would be time to talk later. I haven't figured that one out yet.

This day however, starting from the Lentini to Buccheri portion of the trip, was different for some reason. Maybe it was because we both knew that our journey together through paradise would soon be coming to an end; or maybe it was because our friendship had matured and deepened, I do not know.

What I know is that from the start of the morning, Vita was animated, glowing, happy, and in a great place. I interpreted this as she was much more relaxed since her responsibilities with her clients were finally coming to an end, and she enjoyed my company a bit more too. Something was different on this day I thought.

In any case, as we started our decent up the mountain on this narrow two lane, winding mountain road. The Magic Carpet slowly climbed the hill…past citrus trees which were the only thing we could see. Orange, lemon, mandarin trees were everywhere…on both sides of the road…as far as the eye could see. On gently rolling slopes, down the valleys, and on the sides again of smaller hills, thousands and thousands of citrus trees…and their magnificent colors…surrounded us.

I could see by the look on Vita's face that she was a bit confused. I had told her about the olive trees and we had not yet seen a single one.

As we turned a sweeping corner and as I down -shifted the Magic Carpet in order to prod it to climb yet another approaching steep incline, the scenery changed instantly, as if someone had pressed a clicker on a TV remote control and changed the channel.

Before us, amidst a sweeping panorama of beauty and bounty, appeared the magical olive trees of Buccheri. Thousands and thousands of them. All loaded with olives too. This is why I came, it was harvest time in Buccheri and I wanted to share this special time with Vita.

Silence again overcame us as we witnessed the emerging indescribable beauty of the mountain. Vita said something at this time that floored me for the first time today. There would be more statements later in the day that floored me, but this was the first.

"Alfred," she said "I love this place."

Let me quickly tell you about Vita and the word "love." She would never use that word as an adjective like Americans do. This was the very first time that I heard her say this word while describing a place. Her emphasis too was astounding. She elongated the word "love" for special emphasis. She said this while gazing out the window, as if she was thinking this thought, but verbalized it somehow. I was happy to hear that, I have to tell you the truth.

Finally, after a twenty minute drive through this paradise, we entered the town. This was another completely different visual experience. There are two sections of Buccheri, the old section with its narrow cobblestone streets barely wide enough for my Punto to fit through, and the new section…which would be old by American standards, for sure, but certainly picturesque in any case.

Driving up the narrow cobblestoned roads we were stunned to see one sweeping view of the valley below after another. Vita asked that I stop the car, which I did, and she hopped out.

Climbing a low wall overlooking the valley below, she framed her photo shots like an expert. Her artistic eye capturing any image dwarfs mine, so when she sees an image, I pull the car over. Getting back in the car, she repeated the phrase. "Alfred, I love this place."

She was excited…borderline animated. She was very much out of character on this day. From the onset, her face had been aglow, and this place made her happy. Winding down one road, we ended up into a small cobblestoned line plaza with townspeople milling about… quintessentially Sicilian, I thought to myself.

I rolled the window down and pulled next to a dapper looking gentleman who was dressed impeccably and cut a dashing figure… bella figura…if you know what I mean…on a Tuesday morning, no less. I asked him if he knew where we could buy some excellent quality olive oil.

He smiled at me as he puffed elegantly on his cigarette "Wait here, let me get my son" he said…in perfect English!

When his son came out, his son, also in perfect English, told me that his dad had just moved back here from the states…the Bronx to be exact…and that his name was Antonio and that he was born in the states but had returned to Buccheri a few years ago to open his little espresso bar, find a wife and settle down.

He had sent for his father, and now they were re-united. The story gets better: He also helps part time his good friend by the name of Nicotra who worked at an *oleificio*…a place where the oil is bottled… and he offered to take us there! Wow! What luck! "This place has the best oil in the whole area" he said. "Come, I will get in you car and show you where it is. You will love this oil."

Off we went.

As it turns out, I was familiar with the oil that we bought at the *oleificio.*

The oil was the most spectacular oil that I tasted since I last bought it by the pallet eight years ago when I was importing oil into America from this neck of the woods. I had found the oil maker who makes the oil that three of the four former partners who I used to do business with now use. Wow!

Vita was a little surprised as she saw Mr. Nicotra pour a little amount in small cups for me to sample and to select which one I wanted.

This is oil made from the fabled olives of the mountain of Buccheri...the Iblei Mountains...and this was D.O.P olive oil....a government certification that the olives are grown and produced from this mountain. As a result, the taste of the oil was superb...the acidity rate of this oil was .05%...practically perfect...the color grass-green, the bouquet heavenly...and the finish simply outstanding. I have sampled many varieties of oil over a twelve year career here as an importer, and this oil is absolutely top of the line stuff.

Here we were on the fabled Iblei Mountain...700 meters above sea level...sampling one of the world's best oils. Poor Vita did not know what to make of it. Lithuanians do not sip olive oil like cognac. Like normal people, they use it on salads, fish, and meat...things like that. Her face grimaced when she took a sip of oil from the sample cup. I thought the whole scene hilarious as I knew what was coming. The finish burns the throat a little and is the sign of great oil. As she swallowed the oil, her face contorted a whole bunch!

Mr. Nicotra ended up hand filling two one-liter cans for us, one for Vita's father and the other to bring to the states for myself. After chatting a while with this great person, we headed back to Antonio's bar for an espresso before we left town.

By the time we returned to the bar, word had circulated that an "American lawyer" had come into town, and a few people stopped by to chitchat with me. Everyone was very friendly and I will go back there now as often as possible. I really love this place.

On the way down the mountain, Vita was gazing at the wonderful scenery that continued to unfold before our eyes.

Then she said something that floored me a second time.

"I can live here", she said. "I really could."

Wow. So far, the road trip has gotten off to a great start, I thought.

Part Three: Gallivanting to Pachino and Portopalo

I do not think either one of us wanted to leave Buccheri. We both left feeling that there was a lot yet to explore and experience there, not so much of the social side but more on metaphysical side. It was far and away the most calming and tranquil place that we had visited on all trips. The ride down the mountain was a wistful one and we remained silent as we travelled down the mountain. Neither of us wanted to miss a single visual.

Vita found Paul Schwartz' and Mario Grigov's great album on the iPod named *Aria* and its haunting New Age interpretations of great opera pieces of music fused the experience together on that brilliant sunny morning.

We headed now toward Noto, although at this point that was not our destination. We were heading dead south toward Pachino and then Portopalo as today I wanted to treat Vita to one of my favorite fish restaurants.

We found the meandering route 287 lined with lava-stone walls and enjoyed the ride through Palazzolo as we drove deeper into southern Sicily.

Through the lovely areas of Villa Vela, Castagna and San Corrado di Fuori we traveled at a leisurely pace and admired the non-stop beauty that surrounded us at every twist and turn of the road. This was a portion of the trip that again silence was best accompanied by the haunting melodies that we were enjoying. Cerebral music was appropriate at this time, and Vita played *Masters of Chant* on the iPod. This CD is really Gregorian music set to modern tunes. Simon and Garfunkel's *Scarborough Fair* provided wonderful accompaniment on this portion of the trip.

Skirting Noto we followed the indications now toward Pachino

I always loved this part of Sicily.

About a decade ago, I had purchased a beach house down in this neck of the woods that I humorously wrote about in *The Reverse Immigrant* and *Gaetano's Trunk*.

As we headed closer to the Ionian Sea, the terrain underwent a dramatic change.

Lush vegetation gave way to fairly rocky terrain and huge agricultural farms. We were heading into the area known far and wide for its small cherry tomatoes…the famed tomatoes of Pachino. The area also had wonderful olive oil which is grown under arid conditions. And of course, everyone in Sicily knows about the sumptuous and delicious melons and wine from this area.

As we got closer to Pachino, huge white plastic growing chambers …little mini-Quonset huts which housed the fabled tomatoes and melons…were everywhere. The ride through this area was relaxing, and hardly any traffic was present on this day.

One thing we did talk about on the way down was the olive oil that we had purchased back in Buccheri. I had taught Vita the rudiments of how to make olive oil, but the small place in Buccheri was really a bottler of oil, and not a true olive oil making facility. She wanted to see how olive oil was made.

As I was talking to Vita about this subject, Vita said to me while pointing to a passing building "Do you mean like that one? Let's turn around and see." She had pointed to a sign that said "O*leificio*" and had found an olive oil pressing facility.

We knew we had passed a real *oleificio,* because the sweet scent of pressed oil filled the air. I turned the Magic Carpet around, parked the car, and we entered the facility like we owned it...pretending that we knew what we were doing. We just walked right in.

Local farmers were there with olives from their farms that they had picked and stored in huge five feet wide by four feet deep plastic olive containers. This was their crop from their farm and here they could do two things with it: sell the olives to others as a pre-set price per kilo or get it pressed and take the oil with them in fifteen gallon stainless steel kettles which they could later bottle and sell it.

Approaching the first section of the olive oil making machine, we watched as one of the huge plastic tubs was lifted and gently poured into the first part of the machine. Here any small leaves and twigs were shaken off by the vibrating portion of the machine which did an excellent job of cleaning them. Next, they entered a conveyor belt and which led to a second machine which gave them a quick bath… in fresh water…and then placed immediately placed back on another machine to dry off. Too much moisture is not good for olives…the more moisture, the higher the rate of acid in the oil, and the higher their rates of acid, the more bitter the taste. The olives had a quick in and out thing with the water and were quickly dried.

From this machine they were transported by conveyor belt to the hydraulic press...which pressed everything....skin, olive, pit.... into a mushy substance. It looked like wet oatmeal by the time it was through with this process. Not very appetizing at all.

However, the next step was the crucial one: the mucky and gooey substance was placed in another machine and "pressed" by mechanical means. Literally, the oil was pressed out of the muck. The oil went one way; the muck went another way.

The olive oil that was yielded flowed into another device and ultimately into the stainless steel fifteen gallon containers.

This olive oil would then be taken away and it would ultimately either be filtered and bottled...or left "unfiltered" and bottled.

Either way, it was heavenly.

This region's olives were different that Buccheri's olives. The Iblei olives from Buccheri are mythical. These olives were merely spectacular in quality.

By the way, Sicilian olive trees yield over ten times that of olives trees from other parts of Italy...did you know that? They are highly regarded in all Europe...more than the "famed" Tuscan olives, in my opinion.

Vita was fascinated as she watched the process, and asked many questions. She actually was animated and photographed each step of the production flow. It was a great learning experience for her, but now it was time to leave.

I wanted to treat her to lunch in Portopalo, and my stomach was grumbling, so off we went.

Part Four: Lunch at the fabled El Faro Restaurant.

Portopalo is known for its harbor, its fish markets, its fish restaurants and its sheer and utter beauty. I found this gem of a town years ago and frequently travel to this far away place and one restaurant here kept reverberating in my mind: El Faro Restaurant.

However, I had forgotten its name and the address.

While we were driving down to the area, I called my law partner Massimo who had accompanied me here many times but he too had forgotten the name. However, a call back five minutes later secured the name and address. He had goggled it for us. Google Italia had come through for us.

Portopalo is sandstone white in color…bright, baked, and lovely. In the summer, it is very hot because the Sahara winds from Africa blow here and bake the place. During these hot summer months nothing moves from 2PM to 4PM…literally the whole town goes into hibernation. I knew that as I glanced at my watch because I wanted to make sure that we found the restaurant before it closed for the afternoon siesta.

Which we did.

I recognized a few places as we drove toward the restaurant and a woman who was sweeping the sidewalk nearby gave us final instructions as to where the place was located. We found it in plenty of time.

Therese the owner greeted us. Since the tourists had long since departed by this mid-October date, we had the restaurant completely to ourselves.

We ordered a half liter of vino bianco locale…the local white wine…the first of two that we enjoyed that afternoon, and began chatting with Theresa.

She suggested that she make us a selection of various fish appetizers and also suggested the "spigola"…local white fish as a main entry.

In short order, the table with full with a vast array of fish …from fresh sardines and anchovies in oil to shrimp, calamari, cozze (mussels), small pan fried white fish of which I do not know the name, squid…you name it…if it was in the sea that morning, it was now on the table as an appetizer.

Looking at the huge assortment of fish in front of us I thought to myself that these would be main courses in any American restaurant and the bill for this portion of the meal alone would be over $150.00… not including the wine. What a feed, I thought to myself.

Our conversation was lovely over lunch.

Vita would be leaving in a matter of days, and I was beginning to feel melancholy over her departure. We have developed quite a bond of friendship. I was attached to her by this time is the best way that I can describe how I was feeling.

Dante had had his Beatrice as his inspiration, and now I had mine. Over the five months since we had first started our travels together, Vita had become my Beatrice. Thus, I was (a) attached to her and (b) she had become my Beatrice, and I was a little sad that she was leaving.

We talked about family, life Lithuania…everything and anything really …except her leaving in a few days. The meal could very easily have slipped into a somber event, but we were both intent on making this day the best day of all our road trips, and by the second liter of white wine, we were just fine.

By the time the spigola came as the main course, we merely nibbled on it…we were both stuffed…and I ended up taking most of it home.

The lunch that day was a special one. Sicily and Vita were now interwoven in my memory banks, and I knew that forevermore I could not go to any of the scores of places that we had visited over our five months together without her image popping into my mind's eye. I remember thanking the Good Lord for this opportunity that He bestowed on me.

I always realized that while I do not what the future holds, I know who holds my future. I know that He holds my future and it was Him that put me here at this time. Why, I do not know…but that was for Him to know. I silently thanked Him for what was turning out to be a glorious day.

By the time the book is published, Al Faro will have moved to a new location. I promised Theresa that I would let you know where it would be: Al Faro da Corrado, Via Esonzio, tel; 0931.842772 and the web site; Simply the best fish restaurant in Sicily.

Part Five: Playful Activities at the Port.

The port of Portopalo is beautiful and I wanted to show Vita how beautiful it was. Years ago, my friend Saro Messina took me here early one morning to watch the fish auction. Every morning the fishermen auction their catch to restaurants, markets, stores…and it was fun to watch.

By noontime the port is quiet as the fishermen rest for the next night's work.

We pulled up to the docks and Vita jumped out of the car and started skipping ahead of me. This was so not Vita…who usually is the epitome of self-control and decorum. She looked great on this day. She had on a black summer weight dress and boots, along with jewelry and looked beautiful. I suggested that I take a photo of her by the dock against the backdrop of the port.

As it turns out, we practically did a photo shoot.

I photographed her time and again …and she did likewise with me. In one series of pictures, she wanted to jump in the air and for me and for me to get the shot. After several practice pictures I was able to take very good photos of her jumping for joy. Maybe it was because her work was done with her clients after five months of hard work, or maybe she was enjoying the companionship of a good friend, but the fifteen minutes that we wandered the dock were again a trip highlight.

Wanting to memorialize the event, I stopped a passing car that was driving by the dock an asked the driver if he would take a picture of us. He gladly obliged, and both pictures came out terrific. There are only eight of pictures of the two of us together….ever. Of the five hundred images we had gathered over five months of travelling, we have only eight images together.

When I posted them then next day on my Facebook page, and she did the same to hers, many of our friends commented on them. It was great.

It was a special time in a brilliant and picturesque setting on a mid-October fall day in Sicily. If the feeling that I had at that moment could be bottled and sold, I would sell a million of them, I thought.

Now, it was time to leave…we were going to Marzamemi, and that was going to be an experience…for sure.

Off we went.

Part Six: Marzamemi: The Piazzetta and Some History too

Marzamemi is perhaps the most popular tourist destination in southern Sicily.

Its vast beaches, many hotels, and warm climate make it a destination for Italians and Europeans from all over. Its International Film Festival, and other festivals held throughout the summer have been gathering a lot of attention lately and the last ten years and it has really become a popular vacation spot.

I can see why.

We enjoyed the short ride from Portopalo to Marzamemi…only a few kilometers away, and since the gorgeous Ionian Sea surrounded us, the Bob Marley's CD was the perfect accompaniment to this spot. Technically, Marzamemi is a borough of Pachino, so we were in the same general area as we had been all day.

Many things were open when we arrived but it was obvious to us that the tourist season was at its end. Only a handful of tourists wandered about, which was terrific for us. I had heard many things about Marzamemi: First, that the main piazza located right on the sea, called the *Piazzetta* was a wondrous and romantic thing to behold, and also that this was the place where the "*Mattanza*" used to occur two times a year many years ago.

While I knew little about what this was except from second hand sources, I did know that the word "mattanza" was Sicilian dialect for the word "massacre", so naturally I was interested in learning as much as I could.

We found an excellent parking space next to the *Piazzetta*. As I first walked to the *Piazzetta*, my mind flashed to Mexico or Spain or Spanish California. I was standing in the middle of a wonderful and beautiful old Spanish style plaza…sun baked and huge…with a church in the background, benches on which to sit, shops in which to browse, a cobble-stoned way with more shops that lead to the port lined with many boats.

It was picture postcard beautiful on this sunny October day, and the both of us were thrilled as we explored the area.

Not knowing much about the place, I decided to find a local and get caught up on its history. A nice elderly gentleman was walking by and I stopped him and we began to chat. In fifteen minutes of speaking to me in Sicilian dialect, he taught me more than any touristic guide could possibly have.

He was born in Marzamemi and experienced everything that he told me, as his house…inhabited by generations of his family who were fisherman before him… had taught him. Since he detected that I was an American-Sicilian, and since it was 5PM on a beautiful and warm Sicilian day, and he had nothing to do he told me, he would teach me.

Which he did.

He told me that many people had occupied the area starting from the Greeks, Romans, and Arabs especially, and more recently the Spanish. As a matter of fact…pointing to the port filled with all sorts of sea worthy boats just steps away, he explained that the word Marzamemi was an Arabic word which meant "small port."

He told me that nowadays tuna eggs or roe (called bottarga) and other tuna related products are still popular here…but not nearly as they were years ago, during its heyday. Today, the area is also know for its melons, wine, oil, and its popular summer Folk Festival, Film Festival and Fish and Wine Festival, which are held at different times during the summer. "Troppa confusione" he said…Too much confusion… because tourists flocked to those events.. I made a mental note that next summer I would return.

Pointing to an abandoned building exactly right on the water's edge yet very well preserved, he said to me "here is where they were processed" and then pointing to another building marked by a huge chimney nearby he said "and there is where they were cooked."

Then he explained to me all about the *"Mattanza."*

The Mattanza was the practice of mass killing migrating blue fin tuna as they passed twice a year to their breeding grounds by trapping them with nets and killing them which special spears. The *Mattanza,* had long stopped (he told be that it stopped when he was a little boy… maybe in the early 1950s or so…he could not remember). The killing of the tuna had been so effective that the blue fin tuna had become an endangered species, and the practice was stopped by the authorities.

It had gone on previously for generations. Twice a year, in late spring…usually sometimes in May and then again in late June… fisherman had discovered that thousands of tuna would pass by a low lying inlet not too far off the port. Huge nets were put where the tuna would pass by and when they did, they were snared in the netting.

They were then dragged back to port where the *mattanza* would take place…literally they would be killed by spears with a special hook on them in a manner that had remained unchanged for many years.

As I looked at the port while he was describing the massacre, I envisioned the whole thing. I saw in my head the bloody tuna being hauled in, fishermen with cigarettes dangling out of their mouths grabbing them by hand and throwing them on the cobblestone way, where they were transported into the nearby building for "processing"...whatever that meant.

He told me that once processed in the facility...some were smoked, other placed in bags and sold...most of them were packed in ice in the twentieth century and sold to the Asian markets....but the residue of the tuna was also valuable...the tuna oil...was sold locally.

Today, limited and legitimate fishing still occurs, although highly regulated. Now, when a captain of a ship catches a tuna, the name of the boat and his name is registered and the quantity of tuna is tightly controlled. However, the aura of the massacre of long ago gave way to other more attractive and desirable things as the decades past, and now the *mattanza* has entered into the folk lore of the area.

As I gazed around me, all I saw was a beautiful place. Unsuspecting tourists probably do not know this part of its history, but both Vita and I were fascinated and now we knew. Vita had taken some great images that I later posted on my blog and I enjoy looking at them to remind myself what a glorious time we had and what a glorious place this is.

We finished this portion of the trip by sitting in an outdoor bar for half an hour having a drink and engaging in pleasant conversation. As far as I knew, the road trip was now concluded, I would drop Vita off at her hotel, say good bye to her and be very sad that she was leaving Sicily.

I think the sadness was beginning to show through to her and she asked me what was wrong. I told her that I wished the road trip wasn't ending and that the day could start all over again.

She said to me "Well, it doesn't have to, Alfred. It is kind of early still. Would you like to go to Noto now?"

Noto? That's wasn't on out itinerary, I thought to myself...then again, a trip to Noto would extend the trip, right? Hmmm....I thought to myself.

As was the case with every time that Vita had asked if I wanted to go someplace with her, a one word answer was all it too.

"Sure" I said.

I paid the bill and off we went to find Noto.
I was happy again.

Chapter Twenty-Seven

Off to Noto and the Big Surprise

Dusk enveloped us as we traveled the lonely road from Marzamemi to Pachino and then from Pachino to Noto.

The setting sun coupled with the unlit two lane road had made me alert and careful and the Magic Carpet was really paying attention to the terrain. Vita has uplifting music on the iPod so I would not fall asleep.

I also was a little worried because the needle on the Magic Carpet was really low, and I need to find a gas station pretty quick. I figured I had about 30 miles left in the tank, so I was watching that needle closely..

Passing on this road earlier in the day, I knew that the Ionian Sea was on my right and field after field of crops were on both sides of us, but the view was hidden by the approaching nightfall. It did not look like I would hit a gas station for at least twenty miles, so I was a little nervous.

"I love Noto." Vita told me, trying to distract me. "I have been there many times with my clients and that is why we did not go before… You will love it too," she said.

My knowledge of Noto was in fact limited. While I had zipped past it over the years going here and there, I never took the time to climb the hill and check the place out. I was eager to see it, even though it was dark. What people had told me was that the buildings there were great and it was a popular tourist destination and that in the evening everyone goes there.

"Nighttime is the best time to visit," said Vita. "The town is all lit up, and things are beautiful." she said. "I know a great gelateria that we can have dessert after we walk around a bit."

Noto is located high on a hill about 30 miles west of Siracusa and is situated actually on a plateau overlooking the beautiful Asinaro Valley.

This area has sweet olive oil, almonds and hazelnuts, and great meats too.

As was the case of all these cities, Noto had initially a huge Greek influence, thanks to its close proximity to Siracusa, but over the millennia other invaders had enjoyed her bounty as well....Romans, Arabs, Normans and Spanish all occupied this area at one time or another. Today, there is a distinctly Spanish aura to the town...and of course, a huge Baroque set of building and streets that will knock your eyes out.

Roberto later told me that the olive oil from this part of the province was his favorite... light and delicate, and I regret not picking some up later that evening. I would later have a bottle in my hand, but since I already had a liter of liquid gold from Buccheri with me, I did not want to take a chance of transporting two liters of olive oil in my luggage with me when I returned to the states. Regretfully, I put it back.

I also knew that Noto was the epi-center of the earthquake that had hit Sicily off the coast in 1692 that wiped out most of the eastern seaboard. From accounts that I read about the earthquake, Noto was nearly destroyed and many killed.

Over the centuries, it has been painstakingly re-built, and now I can say this: It truly is one of the prettiest Sicilian towns...on that score I agree with Vita. As for it being my favorite town...I needed at this point to spend more time there, but it is just a joyous place to wander about.

Vita directed me up the steep incline and found us a parking place on the street where the *Giardini Pubblici*...Public Gardens is located. As I parked the Magic Carpet and looked for a place to purchase a parking ticket, I instantly liked the place. First of all, the gardens were an island of tranquility in the center of a small town. A very good sized green and natural space I may add covered with trees, benches, walking paths with many townspeople just walking about, chatting, and enjoying their evening.

I envisioned this scene taking place here for centuries. It was calm, peaceful and beautiful.

The main thoroughfare reminded me of the Corso Umberto in Taormina. Like Taormina is has a huge arch-type gateway called the *Porta Reale*. It reminded me of a Roman arch...tall, rounded, just beautiful. Vita's camera takes excellent pictures during the nighttime, so she was trying to get the right picture framed, which she did.

Shops...elegant shops...lined both sides of the *Corso Vittorio Em-*

manuele...just like Taormina. However, I was impressed by the light color of the buildings, and things seemed taller than Taormina too. The big difference, of course, is that there is no sea view from Noto... it is inland...but the beauty of the Corso amazed me as I walked up the pedestrian –only street.

We walked past the *Piazza Immacolata* and the *Church of Saint Francis* and I think I counted seven gelato shops along the way. We had decided to visit only one church but we also decided to wait a bit before selecting one. We were going to walk the length of Corso Vittorio Emmanuele and then would decide which one to visit.

I was surprised at how much Vita knew about Noto...tonight she was the tour director, I thought to myself, and I was enjoying the private guided tour.

We walked through other sweeping and beautiful squares and plazas, and by now the names were bouncing off my head. I made a mental note that the next time I came here I would study up on the place first, although the piazza with the municipal offices...which was hosting a political event where throngs of people were sitting on the steps listening to an animated speaker talking about government unjustness (isn't that the case everywhere)... was also a very interesting experience.

Vita and I had our last two pictures taken by the street that hosts the annual *Festival of Flowers* ever year in late spring. The entire street is closed off and a blanket of flowers...designed by local artisans...is installed up the length of the street and thousands come from miles around to celebrate this event.

Again I made note to return to see this place during this fiesta.

We meandered up and down several parallel side streets and I was just so impressed with the outstanding Baroque architecture that I saw. With each passing step, with each interesting building and corner I crossed, Noto was rapidly climbing up my list of personal favorites.

We wandered the streets looking at things for over two hours. Now exhausted and still having a ninety minute ride back to Naxos, we decided to have a gelato at the *Café Sicilia* one of the town's most famous gelaterias, and head home.

First, however, we stopped and visited the *Church of Santa Maria* and I am glad we did.

This small and holy place had a breathtaking mural on the ceiling and I comforted myself in knowing that by waiting and choosing this place for me to say my prayer of thanks was the right decision.

Walking back the Corso, we sat at *Café Sicilia* and I enjoyed Gelato di ananas (pineapple gelato) which was great. As usual, Vita sampled about ten different chocolate-flavored gelatos before making her selection of a vanilla and chocolate gelato that she said was also delicious.

By this time, it was almost nine o'clock at night. Out trip had started thirteen hours earlier, and we had done the equivalent of a week's research during this time. We did so many things; we saw so many place, that this road trip had turned out to be the most special of all. It would take me days to process and analyze it all before I could write words about it....as is always the case.

Thinking back that just five months ago I had met Vita, and also realizing how our friendship had grown and how much I had learned about myself, and my Sicily at the same time simply by gallivanting with Vita all over the place, I wanted to thank her.

Well, I tried to thank her, in any case.

I had to watch every word that I said to her. The emotional impact that Vita had on me far outweighed the emotional impact that I had on her.

This I knew from the beginning. Still, a five month friendship of the heart and mind was coming to a close. She would be off to India, Thailand, Spain working with her clients and I would be shortly returning to America to teach at my beloved law schools for several months before coming back here again.

Our time gallivanting around the Sicilian countryside would be over in ninety minutes and I was a little choked up about it internally.

Funny thing about women; they read men far better than men read women. Casually finishing her gelato and taking a sip of her water bottle, she said.

"There is nothing to be sad about, Alfred. I will go home to Lithuania for two months, and then go to India, and before you know it, I might be back here next year."

Thinking back to the first time I had met her, and thinking back to how brashly (and stupidly) I had asked her to marry me (I think it was a joke, then maybe it wasn't...I have to mull that one over), I decided to take another flyer.

You remember what a flyer is, don't you? A flyer, as I described at the beginning of the book, is when you ask a question knowing full well what the answer is before you ask it.

I was going to take a flyer. My last flyer with Vita. A desperation, Hail Mary pass type of flyer with only five seconds left in the game... which was the length of the car ride back to Naxos.

"Vita", I said, "if you have two months off before you go to India, why don't you come with me to America? Let me show you Boston, New York, the White Mountains, New England. You can meet Jennifer, Matthew, Catie and the grandkids, and we can have another road trip there. Who knows...maybe you'll have fun in America."

See? That is a flyer. That is a desperation question asked by a guy who does not want the woman in front of him to leave. A desperation heave-ho as they say in the states. Nothing ventured, nothing gained. Years from now, people who study flyers will analyze and dissect the above statement.

The key, I later decided, was the cool manner in which I asked. Cool, calm, collected....in between bites of pineapple gelato. Maybe that was the key. Pineapple gelato. Only God knows for sure.

"Sure" she said. "I will come to America to visit you for a month."

Huh?

Did she say yes? Or in my delusional state, did she say "no" but instead I heard the word "sure"....which was the very word that I would answer her every time she texted me informing me that the next day was a good day for a road trip for her, and was it for me?

"Sure."...she said.

My new favorite word in the English language.

Vita had accepted my invitation to come to the States as soon as I returned, and that was all I heard.

I cannot remember too much about the ride back to Naxos. My mind was a whirlwind of thought and emotion. I knew this: I was going to plan the trip of a lifetime for this woman. I was going to see to it that by the time the month was done that maybe....

Forget it. Let me tell you this: I was very happy camper on that ride back from Noto…my new favorite Sicilian town.

After dropping Vita off, I told Roberto that Vita had accepted my invitation to come to America. I had told him earlier in the week that I was thinking of inviting her.

He smiled. "I know, Beddu" he said. "She told me a few days ago that she had decided to visit you. Surprise." he said, grinning.

Surprise? Surprise? See that is another thing I learned these five months…Sicilians can, in fact, keep a surprise.

In any case, now you know the whole story about me, my voyage of discovery to becoming "*Only Alfred,*" my best friend "*Only Vita,*" out magical time that we had together…the old guy and the beautiful woman….through the magical Sicilian countryside.

I think it is a very nice story.

Don't you?

Well, the first person I am going to thank for this adventure is the Good Lord.

As I said in the book, I do not now what the future holds, but I know who holds the future. This I mean with every molecule in my body.

By the time you read these words, I will be in America, spending time with the kids, grandkids, teaching at the law schools, talking up the Sicilian Project, and mulling over my road trip in America with Vita and what I intend to do about that.

Here is the point: I am glad that you accompanied me on my voyage of discovery. As you can see, I have a second lease on life and I intend to live every single minute as is if it is my last.

Remember what I want on my gravestone too: "Je ne regret rien"…. I regret nothing.

Thank you to my kids, my Sicilian friends, and everyone else who inspired me to write these words.

We all know who that is, now don't we? Thank you Vita…you mean the world to me...

Grazie mille!

Alfred M. Zappalà
Aci Catena, October, 2012